Life in a Three~Ring Circus

Life in a Three~Ring Circus

Essays by Sharon L. Smith and Stephen J. Fletcher

Printed in Canada

The paper in this publication meets the minimum requirements of American National Standard for Information Sciences—Permanence of Paper for Printed Library Materials, ANSI Z39.48-1984. ∞

Library of Congress Cataloging-in-Publication Data

Smith, Sharon Lee, 1954–
    Life in a three-ring circus: posters and interviews / essays by Sharon L. Smith and Stephen J. Fletcher.
        p. cm.
    ISBN 0-87195-151-7
        1. Circus—Indiana. 2. Circus—Posters. 3. Circus performers—Indiana—Interviews.
    I. Fletcher, Stephen J. II. Title.

GV1803 .S65 2001
791.3'0973—dc21
                                                                                    00-047265

Contents

AN EXTRAVAGANT AND POPULAR TYPE OF THEATER, THE CIRCUS HAS BEEN around in one form or another for more than two thousand years, beginning with Rome's Circus Maximus three hundred years before the time of Christ. Variations of the circus live on in America—from the theatrical Cirque du Soleil and Circus Circus to the Shriner's Circus, Clyde Beatty–Cole Brothers Circus, and Big Apple Circus all the way down to youth, amateur, and modest-size traveling shows.

The circus still thrives in America, despite the time-consuming attraction of television, movies, spectator sports, and the Internet. Why has it survived? What does the circus have that other entertainment lacks? A very simple answer is that only the circus allows its audience to watch talented artists interact with dangerous animals and perform life-threatening feats; only the circus has clowns that interject their silly antics when we can't stand the suspense any longer. All this and theater too! Flamboyant costumes along with music, smells, and bright lights add a uniquely artistic flair to the on-the-spot excitement of the American circus.

But part of the appeal of the circus is our memory of it. We loved going to the circus with our parents, and we take our children to see it when they are old enough; they will in turn no doubt take their children to see the circus, and so it will go on. The art, pageantry, and excitement of the circus evoke childhood memories from audiences across the country, whether they are urban dwellers in New York City or farmers in Indiana. Whoever we are, and whatever our experience, we love the circus. It is this unifying memory of the American circus—and Indiana's role in creating it—that this book attempts to understand.

The American variation on the circus has its roots in late-eighteenth-century Britain. Retired British cavalry officer Sgt. Maj. Philip Astley entertained London audiences in the 1760s by riding his horse Duke Walter with one foot on the saddle and the

The Circus in Indiana

by Sharon L. Smith

other on the horse's head. Astley combined trick riding with juggling, rope dancing, and tumbling acts in his open-air equestrian shows, and he also incorporated clown acts into his circus, borrowing them from the London theater circuit. Astley was the first to introduce the ring to the circus: as he practiced his trick riding, he discovered that the centrifugal force operating in a forty-two-foot-diameter ring made it easier to stay on the horse. The forty-two-foot-diameter ring has defined the parameters of circus performance ever since.

One of Astley's students, John Bill Ricketts, came to the Philadelphia Riding School in 1793 to stage the first American circus. Philadelphia newspapers hailed him, announcing to a fascinated public that he would jump from one horse to another through a hoop and "recover his situation on the other side." Ricketts, a cousin of George Washington, traveled from Philadelphia to Albany and Baltimore and added comic dances and tumbling to his routine, along with rope dancing and "great feats of horseman-ship." Ricketts's circus was wildly successful, and by the end of the 1700s the circus was well established in the new United States.

After the War of 1812, permanent horse shows gave way to traveling shows that performed on village greens. Old Bet, an African elephant, contributed to the success of these early exhibitions. Old Bet's owner, Hackaliah Bailey, who purchased her from a sea captain for $1,000, exhibited her in local barns throughout the countryside, and he was so successful at it that he added other exotic animals, thus introducing a new element to the American circus: the traveling menagerie.

There were no zoos in early-nineteenth-century America; the only way people could see a lion or a tiger or an elephant was to visit the menagerie when it came to town.

Traveling menageries and circuses operated separately for a short time, but as the menageries began to add clowns and acrobats to their performances and as the circuses began to travel with wild animals, the two inevitably merged. Out of this combination came another revolutionary addition: in 1833 menagerie cage boy Isaac van Amberg entered a cage containing wild animals, and the audience was riveted. This potentially dangerous interaction between wild animals and their trainers became an important part of the circus in America. Van Amberg was the first person to put his head in a lion's mouth, but unlike the highly skilled trainers we see today, he had no training whatsoever and used brute force to keep the animals from hurting him.

Clowns also became an integral part of the American circus at about this time. In the early days clowns talked to the audience, offering not only comic relief but political commentary, filling the role of court jester rather than serving as the comic slapstick mimes we are now accustomed to. The most popular clown in the early nineteenth century was Dan Rice, whose distinctive costume, including goatee and red-and-white striped coat and top hat, was the inspiration for cartoonist Thomas Nast's famous Uncle Sam. Rice earned a remarkable $1,000 per week and counted celebrities and politicians among his friends; he was so popular with his audiences that he considered running for president. He called on Zachary Taylor to join him on the bandwagon—a wagon for the circus's musicians— and coined the phrase "jump on the bandwagon."

In the middle of the nineteenth century P. T. Barnum added the final touch to the American circus when he integrated the human and animal oddities of his American Museum of New York City into the traveling circus. In his museum Barnum sensationalized giants, Siamese twins, bearded ladies, midgets, and similar displays. Prior to his entry into the circus business his biggest successes came from his promotion of Siamese twins Chang and Eng and the twenty-five-inch-tall Charles Stratton, who Barnum renamed General Tom Thumb.

Hoping to capitalize on Barnum's New York success, Dan Costello and William Coup asked Barnum to join their traveling circus in 1871. When he agreed, the three men followed the then common penchant for long show names and called the resulting traveling circus P. T.

The most popular clown in the early nineteenth century was Dan Rice. He was so popular with his audiences that he considered running for president. He called on Zachary Taylor to join him on the bandwagon—a wagon for the circus's musicians— and coined the phrase "jump on the bandwagon."

Barnum's Great Traveling Museum, Menagerie, Caravan, Hippodrome, and Grand International Zoological Garden. Similar to all the circuses of this era, the show went from town to town in horse-drawn wagons, slogging ten or eleven miles each day through mud. These circuses were referred to as mud shows, and they gave one- or two-night performances in small towns across the country.

Coup, a Terre Haute native, added a second and third ring to the traveling mud show. More important, he reduced the tedium of circus travel by inventing the end-loading process, a revolutionary way of putting circus wagons onto trains. Implementing this new method, circuses increased daily travel distances and were able to expand their territories and reach larger audiences. Combining railroad transport with Joshua Purdy Brown's 1870s invention of the big top, or circus tent, the shows could now move quickly and easily anywhere in the country, requiring only a flat, grassy place near a railroad stop. In spite of the obvious appeal of railroad travel, however, mud shows did not disappear; as late as the 1930s scores of small circuses still traveled by horse- or engine-drawn wagons.

Barnum bought into the idea of using the railroad to move his circus. He and his partners joined forces with James A. Bailey in 1881, forming the Barnum and Bailey and London Circus. This became an enormous enterprise, and its success led several other entrepreneurs to join the circus business. The competition heated up. Some twenty-five major shows were traveling on the railroads by 1890, including the Forepaugh Brothers, John Robinson, Sells-Floto, and Ringling Brothers Circuses, each covering a well-defined region of the United States.

Indiana businessmen got on the circus bandwagon in the 1880s. Bloomington native H. B. Gentry organized a dog and pony show, and the Gentry Brothers Circus grew substantially over the next decade. Originally an open-air show, it moved under canvas in 1891 and bought out a rival show; by 1892 the Gentry brothers had four circuses on the road. All of them used calliopes made by Sullivan and Eagles of Peru, Indiana.

Farther north, livery stable owner Benjamin Wallace of Peru (still pronounced *Pee*-roo by the circus folks in town) joined with his partner James P. Anderson of Columbus, Ohio, in 1884 to present a mud show. The show traveled under the poetic title of Wallace and Company's Great World Menageries, Grand International Mardi Gras, Highway Holiday Hidalgo and Alliance of Novelties. The name eventually became the Great Wallace Circus. Upgrading to railroad transport in the spring of 1886, the Peru-based Wallace Circus soon became one of the largest in the Midwest. Wallace, who by now was known locally as the "circus king," bought out his partner in 1890 and in 1891 purchased the land adjacent to his farm just outside Peru for his winter quarters. The land originally belonged to Miami chief Gabriel Godfroy and was bounded by the Mississinewa and Wabash Rivers.

Circus people today continue to use winter quarters during the off-season, between November and April. There they train acts and animals, build and paint wagons, repair machinery, and prepare themselves for the next season. Wallace soon discovered that his winter quarters at Peru was an ideal site because it had enough land to house and grow feed for the animals and offered direct access to both the railroad and the rivers. He expanded his property and eventually employed five hundred people there.

By the time Barnum died in 1891, the Barnum and Bailey and the Ringling Brothers shows were contending for the spotlight in the circus business, and eventually Bailey and the Wisconsin-based Ringling Brothers waged a bidding war that ended with the Ringling Brothers purchase of Barnum and Bailey in 1907 (though the two shows remained separate entities for the next twelve years). That same year Wallace went into partnership with Jeremiah "Jerry" Mugivan to buy a popular German exotic animal show, the Karl Hagenbeck Circus. The result of this $45,000 purchase was the 1907 debut of the Hagenbeck-Wallace Circus, the flagship show of the many Peru-based circuses. For a time the second-largest circus in the United States, the show toured the country's midsection, from the Rockies to the Appalachians. It offered competition to the Ringling Brothers operation.

DURING THESE EARLY YEARS OF THE TWENTIETH CENTURY, MANY Americans lived far from the city. Even in urban areas, entertainment was limited, and the small mud, medicine, and minstrel shows had a captive and enthusiastic audience. For the same reasons the railroad circuses became the number one entertainment form in the United States during this period. Schools, businesses, and government offices shut down when the big circuses rolled into town; it was like a holiday. With an average ticket price of only ten cents, anybody could afford to go, and everybody went. With such large audiences to motivate and fund them, circuses added acts and animals and vied with one another for top billing.

The Hagenbeck-Wallace Circus was one of the most popular circuses in this competitive market, but Wallace's fortunes soon took a downturn. During the flood of 1913 the Wabash River broke its banks at Peru, and water filled the streets. The flood swept bridges, businesses, and homes off their foundations, killing eleven people and costing the town $2 million in damages. Wallace and his winter quarters alone suffered $150,000 of Peru's total losses, including the drowning of eight elephants, twenty-one lions and tigers, and eight performing horses. Wallace was sixty-five years old, and this disaster signaled the end of his circus career. He sold the Hagenbeck-Wallace Circus to Peru real estate tycoon Charles Edward Ballard.

Ballard moved the show's winter quarters to West Baden Springs, in southern Indiana, and the show did well for several years, employing four hundred staff members and performers and traveling on forty-nine

Brothers and Barnum and Bailey Circus, which made its debut in 1919. Traveling with an astonishing six thousand tons of equipment and a staff of five hundred, this biggest of American circuses traveled the country on eighty railroad cars. The East Coast was its primary territory, and it opened each year in Madison Square Garden in New York City. The ACC, in response to the Ringling success, bought more land and expanded the winter quarters, and over the course of the following seven years it bought the Sells-Floto, Sparks, and Al G. Barnes Circuses, adding many more animals and performers to their shows.

By 1920 the winter quarters at Peru consisted of three thousand acres and was host to five circuses. Combined, these shows were even larger than the Ringling Brothers extravaganza.

railcars. But Ballard had no better luck with his investment than Wallace did. On 22 June 1918 the Hagenbeck-Wallace Circus train crashed just outside Hammond, Indiana. Eighty-six people died, including several star performers. Another 175 people were injured. The train collided with an empty Michigan Central troop train, and blame fell on the engineer of the latter train, who had apparently fallen asleep. In 1918 the federal government was operating all trains in the United States, and because the government could not be sued, the families of the dead and injured made claims for damages against the show itself. Ballard paid for the victims' funerals and settled the personal injury claims out of his own pocket, to the tune of some $1 million. He refused to halt the show in midseason and filled out his performances with acts borrowed from shows owned by Ringling Brothers.

Not surprisingly, the Hagenbeck-Wallace Circus went bankrupt and was sold at auction in December 1918. The winning bidders, at a very low $36,100, were Mugivan and Bert Bowers, owners of the John Robinson Circus and the Howe's Great London Circus. Ballard joined them a few years later as a partner, and the three called their business the American Circus Corporation (ACC). Its headquarters was located at Wallace's old winter quarters in Peru.

The ACC's shows competed with the newly combined Ringling

By 1920 the winter quarters at Peru consisted of three thousand acres and was host to five circuses. Combined, these shows were even larger than the Ringling Brothers extravaganza. During the height of the winter quarters in the 1920s more than fifty elephants wintered in its barns, along with hundreds of cats, bears, and other exotic animals. Between eight hundred and one thousand draft horses, most of them used to pull the several hundred circus wagons on and off the railroad end loaders, were pastured in the fields near the river. All the animals had tenders as well as trainers, and all were fed from feed grown on-site. Maintenance workers, aerialists, animal trainers, acrobats, clowns, and sideshow personnel also lived in the winter quarters, along with their families. The place was self-sufficient: it included staff houses, cookhouses, a barbershop, and a fire department. It was the largest American circus winter quarters ever built. Peru became known as the circus capital of the world.

Each of the five shows, known collectively as the Corporation Shows, toured the Midwest and traveled the railroads to the West Coast, East Coast, and South. The bright yellow, red, and blue of their wagons lent splashes of color to the dusty roads of Peru, and the calliopes sounded their presence for a five-mile radius as the circuses paraded from the headquarters to the railroad station every

CRISTIANI BROS.
3 RING - WILD ANIMAL
CIRCUS

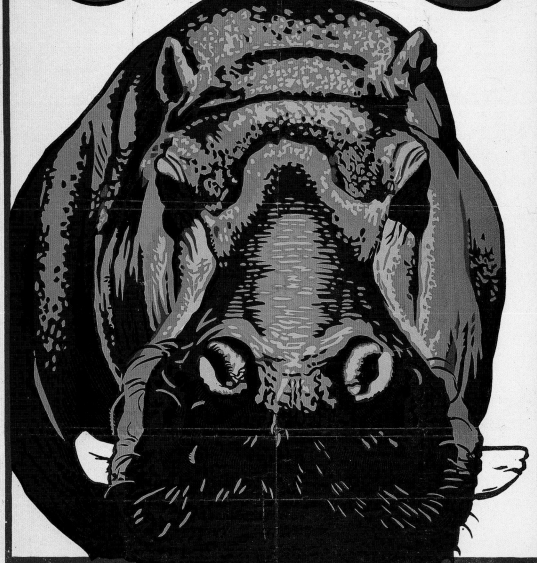

spring and once again every winter when they returned home. People from all over Miami County came to watch the spectacle.

These shows featured the best acts the circus could offer, and they made a memorable contribution to the golden age of the circus in early-twentieth-century America. Many famous performers began their careers working on these shows; some eventually got into films and became household names. Mickey King was launched almost by accident while a ballet girl on the Sells-Floto show; her sister Antoinette Concello ran away from a convent in the 1920s to become one of the famous Flying Concellos, working on the Sells-Floto and Hagenbeck-Wallace Circuses and then with Ringling Brothers. Emmett Kelly developed his hobo persona while working with Otto Griebling on the Hagenbeck-Wallace Circus; Clyde Beatty got his start in 1928 as a cage boy with the ACC-owned Howe's Great London Circus.

IN THE LATE 1920S THE ACC DECIDED TO BUILD ON ITS SUCCESS AND buy out the Ringling Brothers operation. John Ringling—whose "Greatest Show on Earth" was equally popular—was just as determined to buy out the ACC. The two sets of owners met in Peru in September 1929, occupying a room in the Farris Hotel as they negotiated a deal. Legend has it that the buyout was determined by the flip of a coin; all that is known for certain is that Ringling arrived at the hotel carrying suitcases filled with cash. It must have been a dramatic day, with the three ACC executives exchanging glances and Ringling hovering over his money, all of them determined to come away the owner of the biggest circus in America. When the price reached $2 million, the ACC owners decided to fold and gave up their entire operation to Ringling.

Ringling now owned the five circuses with all their equipment. He owned the performers' contracts, and he owned the winter quarters. The performers he had to choose from included the famous hobo clowns Griebling and Kelly, lion tamer Beatty, the remarkable equestrian Cristiani family, and aerialists Mickey King and Antoinette and Art Concello. Under the Ringling Brothers organization he already held the contracts of the acrobatic DeLong sisters, star aerialists Lillian Leitzel and Alfredo Codona, the Flying Wallendas, the Hanneford Riding Troupe, and bandleader Merle Evans.

But Ringling's timing was disastrous. He bought out the ACC one month before the stock market crash of October 1929. He had signed a note with the Prudence Bond and Mortgage Company for the $2 million price of the ACC assets and defaulted on his payments in the aftermath of the crash. In short order the Prudence note for the Ringling organization, including the five Peru circuses, was purchased by Allied Owners, Inc. Ringling retained nominal influence as the conglomerate's president, but Sam W. Gumpertz was now its new general manager.

Despite this stabilizing business arrangement, the Great Depression hit the Peru circuses very hard. The ninety-year-old John Robinson Circus went out for the last time in 1930; in 1932 the Sells-Floto Circus ended, and the Al G. Barnes Circus gave up the fight in 1933. The performers and other staff members lost their jobs, and the equipment sat idle in the barns at the Peru winter quarters. The Hagenbeck-Wallace Circus remained, though, and in 1934 a Peru local named Jess Adkins became its manager. He had the pick of all the out-of-work circus performers and the unused equipment, and he put together a star-studded show that was so successful it outgrossed its parent company, the Ringling Brothers and Barnum and Bailey Circus.

The year 1934 was, however, the last of Peru's golden age. None of the Peru circuses went out in 1936, and because of recession and union disputes, 1938 was a disastrous year throughout the circus business. The Hagenbeck-Wallace Circus fell victim in 1938, going bankrupt on a run to California. The only Indiana circus to survive the 1930s was the Cole Brothers Circus, an offshoot created in 1935 by Peru lion trainer Zach Terrell and manager Adkins. Griebling and Kelly were the Cole Brothers clowns, and Beatty starred in the center ring. With its headquarters in Rochester, Indiana, the show lasted until 1950.

Gumpertz, now managing the Ringling operation, had in the meantime made circus history by ordering John Ringling off the lot during the 1936 opening at Madison Square Garden. Ringling died later that year, and his nephew, John Ringling North, bought out Allied Owners and regained control of the family organization in 1938. With the death of John Ringling, the Ringling family broke into factions, and between the internal pressures, the overwhelming losses of the prior five years, and the continual circus labor disputes, North decided to move out of Peru. For a year or two he kept the Ringling horses at the winter quarters, but in 1941 he sold the property to Emil Schram, an Indiana businessman who was president of the New York Stock Exchange and secretary of the treasury under Franklin D. Roosevelt.

In the aftermath of the sale, North ordered all the equipment left at the Peru winter quarters hauled into the middle of the fields and burned. One hundred forty circus wagons—many of them hand carved and layered with gold leaf, some of them more than fifty years old—were destroyed on the afternoon of 22 October 1941. North did not see this as wanton destruction; for him the equipment was surplus, and it was too much trouble to haul it to Sarasota, Florida, Ringling's main winter quarters.

For five years the Ringling family argued over who would be in charge of the financially troubled organization. In the meantime North streamlined the circus, trying to make up his losses by appealing to what he understood to be trends in American popular culture. He was, after all, now competing with radio and movies, as well as the new technology of television. He replaced many of the old circus staff and recruited new performers from Europe. He stopped using the colorful posters that for many people meant "circus." Ringling Brothers was hit by a string of disasters in the 1940s, including a 1942 fire in Cleveland and the most disastrous fire in circus history, which took place under the big top in Hartford, Connecticut, in 1943.

RAILROAD TRAVEL AND LABOR HAD BECOME TOO EXPENSIVE; THE traveling circus was in deep trouble. In 1956 union pickets at the gate during the Madison Square Garden opening drove the audience away, and labor disputes disrupted performances across the country. Finally, on 15 July 1956 North announced that the traveling Ringling show would close after that evening's Pittsburgh

performance. "The tented circus as it now exists," he said, "is in my opinion a thing of the past." The show did open again in 1957 at Madison Square Garden, but it now performed only in arenas.

While the American railroad circus ended in 1956, Ringling's shift to arenas did not end the tented circus altogether. The old Rochester-based Cole Brothers Circus, for example, was bought by Acme Circus Corporation, combined with the Clyde Beatty Circus, and evolved into the present-day Clyde Beatty–Cole Brothers Circus. Circus Vargas, organized in Hollywood in 1969, began as a motorized show with three trucks and eight animals and now performs in a three hundred-by-two hundred-foot big top that weighs seventeen tons. Featuring fourth- and fifth-generation performing families from more than a dozen countries, Circus Vargas shifted to the European-style one-ring format in 1993 and plays two or three towns a week, setting up on shopping center parking lots or in city parks. As for Ringling Brothers, Israel Feld and two others bought the Ringling Brothers and Barnum and Bailey Circus in 1968. Feld's son Kenneth now runs the Ringling circus, and he also works with illusionists Siegfried and Roy and manages Walt Disney's World on Ice and American Gladiators.

Most present-day small- and moderate-size circuses are run locally, using regional sponsors and advertising to increase ticket sales. The Culpepper-Merriweather Great Combined Circus, a medium-size one-ring circus out of Phoenix, Arizona, offers low-cost performances in fourteen states. Its founders include "Cap" Terrell Jacobs III, the son of a flyer and grandson of the famous cat trainer Captain Terrell Jacobs of Peru. A few of the three-ring shows have found larger sponsors. Of these, the most recognizable are the Shrine-sponsored circuses such as the Hamid-Morton Circus and the Polack Brothers Circus. Local Shrine clubs arrange circuses for their towns, or several Shrine clubs cooperate to arrange a tour throughout a state or region. Five hundred shows are sponsored by the Masonic Order of Shrines every year.

Several shows founded in the past twenty-five years have successfully added modern changes. The Pickle Family Circus of San

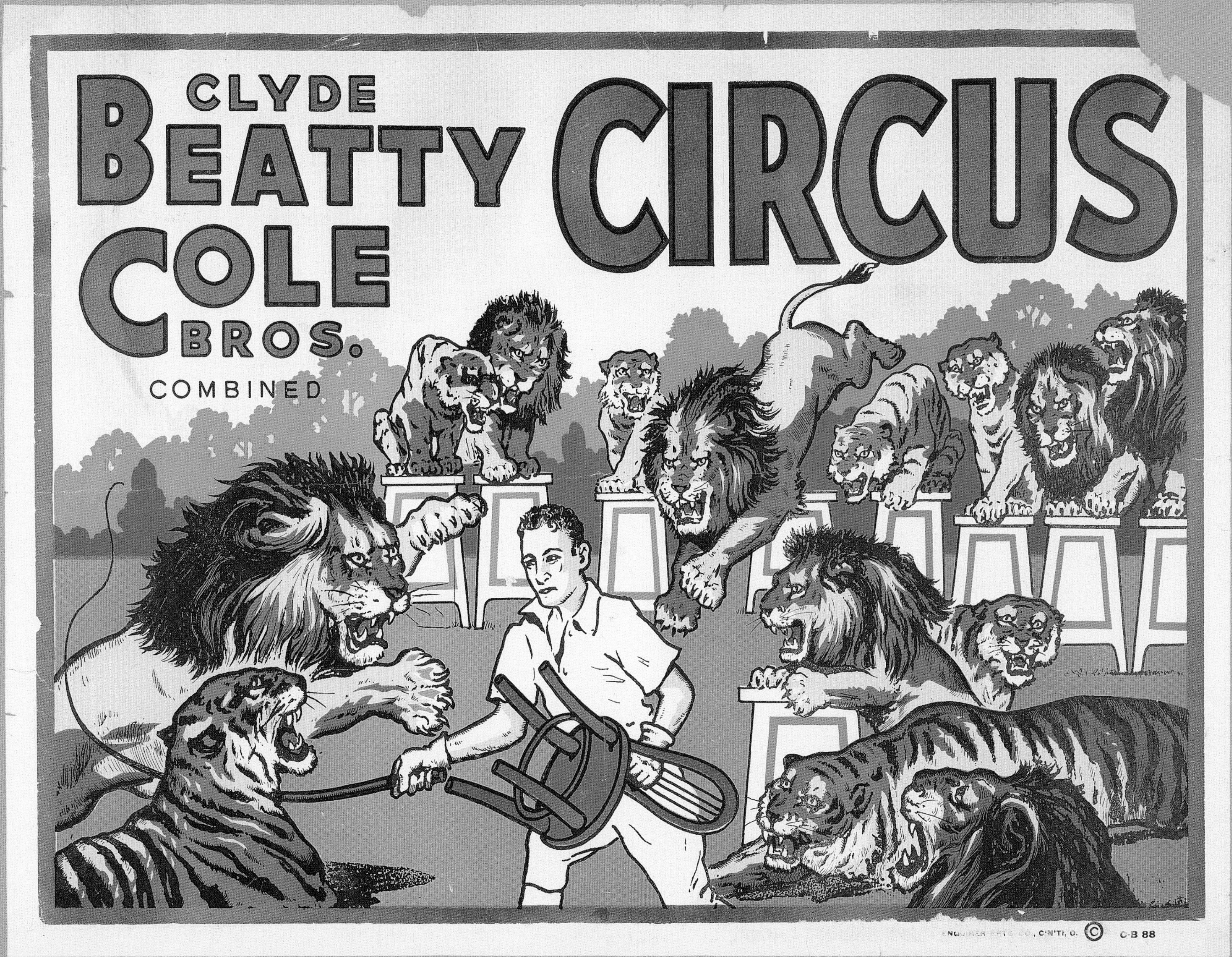
CLYDE
BEATTY
COLE
BROS.
COMBINED
CIRCUS
ENQUIRER PRTG. CO., CIN'TI, O. © C-B 88

Francisco, for example, introduced a modern sound system in the 1970s, adding jazz to the traditional circus music offering. New York's Big Apple Circus started about the same time as a small one-ring circus that was mounted on landfill in Battery Park; it now emphasizes animal acts and performs in one ring under canvas in the larger eastern and midwestern cities.

The circus in America has turned to niche markets, and many have become internationalized, beginning with the money-saving shift back to the European one-ring format. Circuses from all over

festival staff is now two thousand strong and is composed in part of professional circus performers and their families.

The youth of Peru audition and begin training for the amateur circus each May, and they spend long hours learning high-wire acts, acrobatic performances, and trick cycling, among other skills. The circus kicks off with a huge parade through town in mid-July, then over the next several days the young people perform for packed audiences in the downtown Circus City Festival building. The amateur circus has trained several generations of young performers, and some

In 1989 the old Peru winter quarters became home to the International Circus Hall of Fame after a group of Peru circus fans bought out the bankrupt Circus Hall of Fame in Sarasota, Florida. At the core of the Hall of Fame's collection are more than one thousand artifacts and a growing number of original circus wagons.

the world have become much more familiar to American audiences: the Moscow Circus has toured here many times, and Cirque du Soleil of Montreal sets up its distinctive tents every year in the larger North American cities, offering a theatrical, European-style show that features state-of-the-art electronic lighting and music systems, elaborate costuming, and cutting-edge choreography.

Peru should have become simply another of the state's many small towns, but the circus had been there too long. For years Peru had been the winter home of scores of circus people. These folks stayed there after the winter quarters shut down, and their influence on the town's identity and priorities did not go away in 1941 with the animals and equipment. They established families and community ties and considered Peru their home. In 1960 a group of Peru circus families and fans got together and created the Circus City Festival, which each year features an amateur circus starring up to 250 children and young people from Miami County. The Circus City Festival puts all its energies into carrying on the tradition of performances that began during the golden age of the American circus. The volunteer

of them now have professional careers as acrobats, daredevils, aerialists, and clowns. Some have even gone on to earn national and international acclaim.

In addition to spicing up the summer in the Midwest, the Circus City Festival can take considerable credit for providing an example of a successful youth-centered circus operation. Several youth circuses and summer training camps for circus performance have sprung up over the past twenty years. The Circus Kingdom and Circus Kirk are both traveling youth circuses, the former founded by an Evangelical United Brethren pastor, the latter run by the Youth Ministries Division of the Lutheran Church in America. Clown Camp in Wisconsin, Circus Smirkus in Vermont, Ringling Brothers Circus Camp in Florida, and Circus of the Kids, held at the French Woods Festival of the Performing Arts in Hancock, New York, all teach young people the finer points of clowning, juggling, and trapeze work, along with trick cycling and other daredevil stunts. Some of these camps have joined forces with Russian, Latvian, and other European circus training schools, broadening young performers' experience and promoting the American circus in the process.

In 1989 the old Peru winter quarters became home to the International Circus Hall of Fame after a group of Peru circus fans bought out the bankrupt Circus Hall of Fame in Sarasota, Florida. The Peru winter quarters barns are slowly being renovated, and there are plans to construct an educational building on the site to serve schools and other organizations interested in learning the history of the circus. At the core of the Hall of Fame's collection are more than one thousand artifacts and a growing number of original circus wagons. Every summer the Hall of Fame puts on a professional circus, complete with a big top and center ring, scores of exotic animals, and nationally known performers.

Holding three of the most extensive and informative collections of circus memorabilia outside the Ringling Museum of Art in Florida, Peru continues to keep the memory of the old traveling circus alive, while at the same time contributing to the evolving American circus. Both old and new forms of the circus thrive in Peru. Along with the young amateur circus performers who continue to call it home, some of the old Sells-Floto, John Robinson, Hagenbeck-Wallace, and Ringling Brothers performers still live there, and they come out of retirement every once in a while to tell their stories again to a new generation of circus fans.

MANY OBSERVERS OF THE AMERICAN CIRCUS HAVE NOTED THAT advertising was its lifeblood—without adequate publicity audiences would not materialize. Advertising was especially important because circuses played mainly in small towns and usually for only a day. It is not surprising to learn, then, that the largest part of a circus company's budget went toward promotion.

Early American circus advertisements took many forms, including handbills and newspaper announcements. But the most creative and colorful promotional tool was the poster. Beginning in the 1780s printers used wood engravings or woodcuts to produce show posters. In 1790s circus jargon these became known as "bills," drawn from the word handbill. By the 1880s the lithograph was the mainstay of circus poster production, and the posters came to be known as "lithos."

Because wood engravings were expensive, printing companies began generating stock posters, a practice that continued well into the twentieth century. To garner revenue from stock posters, printers created generic illustrations that could be used by any circus. Circus companies selected designs that appealed to them, and the name of the circus was then printed on the versatile stock posters. In contrast to stock posters, circuses also used specialty posters made for specific acts or to highlight the uniqueness of their company.

Circus posters came to be printed on the basis of a standard size, twenty-eight by forty-two inches, commonly referred to as a sheet. Surviving posters, however, rarely measure exactly that size.

Several sheets, each containing part of an overall scene, could be combined to produce a very large poster. A typical billboard, for example, uses sixteen sheets. The largest poster utilizes twenty-four sheets.

The Circus Poster

An Overview
by Stephen J. Fletcher

On the other hand, the smallest poster is the half sheet, which measures twenty-one by twenty-eight inches, or if cut lengthwise into a half-sheet hanger, measures fourteen by forty-two inches. (Again, these sizes are rarely exact.) Similar to the poster format is the card, printed on a heavier paper stock than the poster. Cards typically measure twenty-two by twenty-eight or fourteen by twenty-two inches.

Whether a circus employed stock or specialty posters, it purchased a large supply estimated to last throughout a tour. It wasn't enough, however, simply to put out posters that said the circus was coming to town. A community needed to know where and when the circus would perform. While buying generic posters in bulk minimized the cost, the absence of a published date on the posters also minimized the size of the audience. To solve this problem, circuses used cheaply printed date sheets, which they posted separately or attached to the printed stock of specialty posters. To catch the eye, the date was almost always the largest printed information on the sheet.

Teams of workmen arrived at an upcoming venue a few weeks before the scheduled date. These teams traveled on specially adapted, brightly decorated railroad cars called advance cars, which were coupled to the end of freight trains. The Ringling Brothers Circus, for example, adapted baggage cars or coaches to accommodate a manager's office, bunk beds, storage, workbenches, and a boiler to make steam to cook the paste used to adhere the posters to walls. In the advance car's heyday, Ringling used as many as eight cars, but by the 1940s the Ringling Brothers and Barnum and Bailey Circus operated only one, which by 1950 was supplemented with station wagons. With the help of their automobiles, advance teams covered areas up to fifty miles from the site of the circus performance. In 1955 the

Ringling Brothers and Barnum and Bailey Circus discontinued its use of the advance car altogether.

Overnight, an advance team blanketed a city or town with posters. The manager assigned one man a major street to cover, and he set out with a hod full of posters and date sheets, good enough to cover thirty locations. A real-photo postcard in the Indiana Historical Society (IHS) collections depicts the results of two circus advance teams on one city block in Greensburg, Indiana. Scads of circus posters hang in windows, cling to boards leaning against the Odd Fellows building and to a post across the street, loom overhead on telephone poles, and dangle from the edge of awnings. A multisheet poster sits atop a plain flat-front building. Even the side of a horse-drawn wagon cannot escape the escapade. One notices the prominence of the numbers 8 and 17. All these posters announce the arrival of two circuses, the John Robinson Big Four-Ring Circus on 8 August and the Hagenbeck-Wallace Circus on 17 August 1907. (It was in 1907, incidentally, that Karl Hagenbeck and Ben Wallace combined their shows to form the Hagenbeck-Wallace Circus.)

The posters featured in this book come from a 1968 IHS acquisition and represent several circuses with and without Hoosier ties: Clyde Beatty, Clyde Beatty-Cole Brothers, Famous George W. Cole, Cole Brothers, Cristiani Brothers, Hagen Brothers, Hagenbeck-Wallace, Al G. Kelly

and Miller Brothers, Ringling Brothers and Barnum and Bailey, and Russell Brothers. The book also highlights the work of some of the finest circus poster publishers, many from the Midwest and the Ohio River valley, including the following:

- Ackerman-Quigley Litho Company, Kansas City and New York
- Acme Show Print, Hugo, Oklahoma
- Central Show Printing Company, Mason City, Iowa
- Enquirer Printing Company, Cincinnati
- Erie Litho. and Printing Company, Erie, Pennsylvania
- Globe Poster Corporation, Chicago
- Majestic Poster Press, Los Angeles
- Neal Walters Poster Corporation, Eureka Springs, Arkansas
- Strobridge Litho Company, Cincinnati and New York

To supplement its poster collection, in 2000 the IHS acquired several advertising fliers and samples for stock posters made by the Globe Poster Corporation. A few of these samples matched some of the posters acquired in 1968. With these examples from Globe Poster, one can see differences between the proposed advertisements

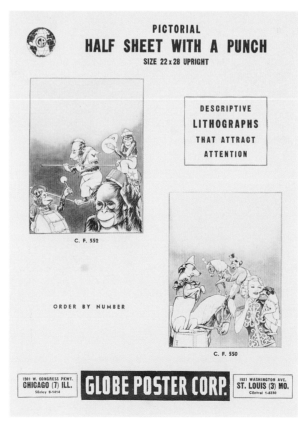

shown to circus proprietors and the final product as seen by gaping children on street corners. These new acquisitions, coupled with the established poster collection, help the IHS keep Indiana's circus heritage alive, and we hope the reproductions in this book convey to the reader a sense of the colorful traditions involved.

LITHOGRAPHED IN BRILLIANT COLORS

C. F. 530

C. F. 531

ORDER BY NUMBER

1501 W. CONGRESS PKWY.
CHICAGO (7) ILL.
SEeley 8-1414

GLOBE POSTER CORP.

1531 WASHINGTON AVE.
ST. LOUIS (3) MO.
CEntral 1-6330

GLOBE'S NEW LITHOGRAPH

6 SHEET IN BRILLIANT COLORS

C. F. 529

NEW LITHOGRAPH

SPECIAL CLOWN ONE SHEET FLAT

C. F. 592

GREAT BILLS FOR WINDOW WORK

C. F. 593

LADY RIDER WITH CLOWN One Sheet Flat

8 COLOR FLAT ONE SHEET THAT DEMAND ATTENTION

633 PLYMOUTH COURT
CHICAGO (5) ILL.

GLOBE POSTER CORP.

1531 WASHINGTON AVE.
ST. LOUIS (3) MO.

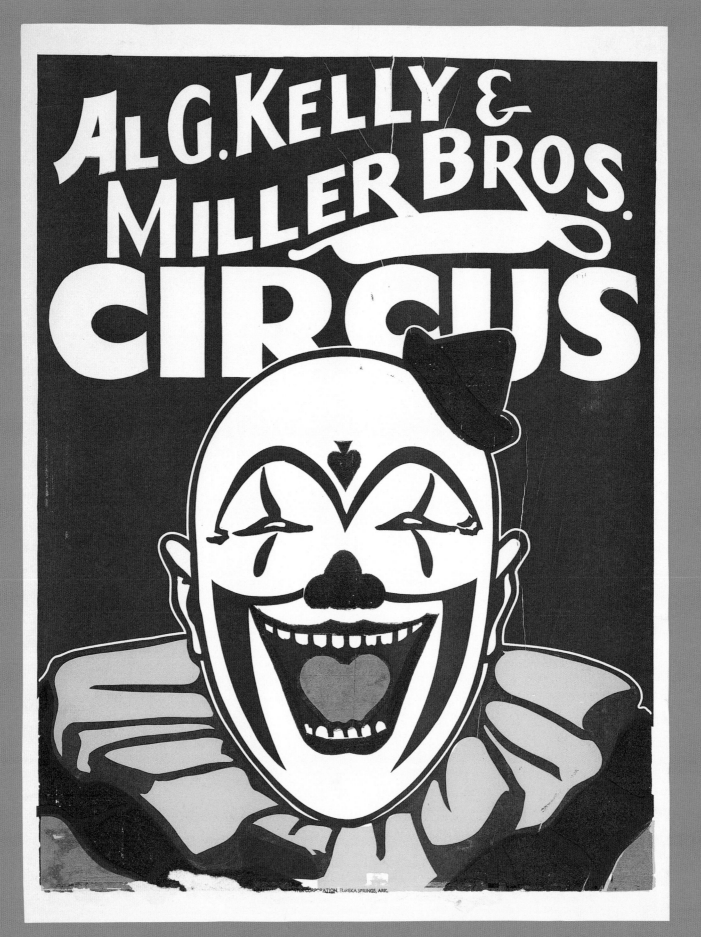

John Fugate

Interviewed by Sharon L. Smith,
with Tom Dunwoody

24 February and 22 March 2000

John Fugate began his circus life as a child clown. As an adult he earned a master's degree in mass communication, but he could never quit the circus entirely. Because of his booming voice he switched to the role of ringmaster in 1979, and as ringmaster he has performed with several of the big circuses across the country. He lives in Peru and acts as the ringmaster and performance director for the International Circus Hall of Fame.

• • • • •

Sharon: When did you start in the circus?

John: I started in Terre Haute when I was six years old. My grandparents raised me, you know, and my grandfather and I were looking for my aunt Ruby Haag, now Ruby Brown. We were looking for her and her dogs, but she wasn't on the lot. This clown was sitting there, making up, and he had his face on pretty much, and my grandfather and I walked by and I stopped. "Wait a minute, Grandpa."

The clown looked at me and he said, "You want to be a

"You want to be a clown?"
"Boy, do I!"

clown?" "Boy, do I!" So I put on the papier-mâché heads and did the walk around. They thought I was a midget because I had this big voice. I did that every summer for ten years, and every circus that came around we would go visit. My grandpa was a cousin to the Timberlakes, and they were circus performers. Somehow it got into my blood. My grandmother used to say, "I don't care if you go to college. If you want to run away and join the circus, go ahead."

I kind of fell in love with the circus right there, right at the Tom Pax Shrine Circus in Terre Haute. Every year we'd go back, and we'd visit with the boss clown—that same clown—who was there from 1950 through about 1960. He was always there.

• • • • •

John: I went off to Indiana University to get a degree, started in the school of music and ended up getting a degree in speech-theater, radio and television. And I never told anyone I did the circus until towards the end. I was kind of ashamed of it, they used to talk about those carny and circus people, and I wasn't going to tell them *I* was one of those carny and circus people!

Finally, I did a class in makeup, and the clown came out of me, and I did this clown makeup. I went down to the Goodwill, and I put together a costume and everything, and I showed up, and they all went, "Holy cow." To say the least, I aced the class, and everyone knew from then on that I had something to do with the circus. "If you need a clown, call Fugate, he'll do it."

I got out of college, and I started going to circuses again. My grandmother kept saying, "Come on, take me to the circus." My grandmother didn't drive. My grandfather passed away the first year out of college. So

we went to see a lot of circuses for three or four years, and I got my master's degree, and I went to work for the Indianapolis Motor Speedway.

• • • • •

John: Now I had a master's degree in mass communication from Indiana State, and I had been at the [Indianapolis Motor] Speedway about six months, and the Shrine Circus came to Indianapolis. A friend of [mine] said, "Here's six tickets for the front row for tomorrow at the Shrine Circus, get your friends and go."

So I took a couple of race drivers, girlfriends, and what have you, and we went, and a guy named Tarzan Zerbini was in the "great cage." Tarzan Zerbini. No whip, no gun, no chair, "The Lord of the Jungle, Tarzan!" He used to ride in on an elephant with big tusks. He'd ride in on that elephant, grab what they call a web, and swing over and drop into the cage. And he's wearing nothing but a loincloth and a wireless microphone hooked into his costume. With an entrance like that, he didn't have to do much else! He was one of the first people to introduce comedy into a cat act. He had lions and tigers and everything in there—about twelve cats.

Afterwards, the race drivers all said, "I want to meet this guy," so we all went backstage, and I bumped into an artist I knew named Robert Weaver. He painted circus people as well as auto racing.

I said, "Where are you from, Bob?" and he said, "Peru, Indiana." And I said, "Oh, circus capital of the world." "How'd you know that?" So we got to talking, and then Bob Weaver and I started going everyplace in the circus together.

• • • • •

John: I came up to Peru in 1972, and by 1976 I was still working at the Speedway in the public relations department and clowning professionally for Tarzan. He and I became close friends. He broke me into the business, he and his father-in-law Joe Bauer.

Sharon: So you were a clown first, even as an adult?

John: Yes. I was clowning with the Youth Circus from about 1976 on, and in 1979 they called me and said, "We're doing a road show at the state museum, right there by the Market Square Arena, on Sunday."

I said, "Yeah, I know, I was going to clown with you guys."

Well, they said, "Could you announce it? We don't have a ringmaster." I did, and the rest, as they say, is history. I think I only clowned once or twice after that. I started announcing, and when Mr. Bauer found out I could announce, he started hiring me.

I'd take a little time here, a little time there, and then in 1980 I left the Speedway and moved to Peru to run the Chamber of Commerce. I clowned very little after that, but I ringmastered a lot. They would fly me in, fly me out, I would do the Shrine show for a weekend, and then fly back, and be back in the office Monday afternoon.

• • • • •

Sharon: What does a ringmaster do?

John: The ringmaster, he's in charge. He's got a tough job. He's on the floor for two hours. He's on the floor throughout the performance. It's his job to make sure that it keeps running smoothly. It's his job to make sure that the audience never knows when there's a mistake or a miscue, or a missed entrance, or somebody gets hurt. He's in charge, it's his job to do all of that.

Sharon: Does he decide who goes on first, and who's in the middle ring?

John: In most cases, the ringmaster is also the performance director and does that. Now at Ringling, they have two people do it, but they have a lot more money, and they can divide it. In the Shrine circuses, usually the performance director and the ringmaster are the same person. However, you always work in concert with the producer. In my case, usually it was Tarzan Zerbini. Now I've worked for Tarzan, the Jordan International Circus, Huber International, Plunkett Family Circus—there are only about four left I haven't work[ed] with. I'm very proud of that, that I've worked with all the big ones.

• • • • •

John: In 1986 we had started chasing the owner of the Circus Hall of Fame [at that time in Florida], and by 1987 we'd bought it. By 1990 we had moved it out to where it is now. I conned Tom [Dunwoody, director of the International Circus Hall of Fame in Peru] into getting on the board, and we've been "putzing" around with this thing ever since—as he says, "living the dream." In 1995 we started doing our show right on the grounds and not moving it around the state. This year will be the sixth year.

Sharon: You're going to have a big cat man this year, somebody special?

John: Yes, Doug Terranova. He does all the animals for Walker TV series [*Walker, Texas Ranger*]. He's an all-around animal behaviorist. He's got about 110 to 115 animals of different species.

Sharon: I wish I could've got a straight answer out of Ruby (see pp. 66–67), how she trained those dogs.

Tom: There's no secret to it, it's psychology, like Pavlov's dogs. A good trainer will watch the animals at play and find out what they do naturally. We had a dog who would smile on command. She did it automatically, and

I would say, "smile," and everybody thought that was a great trick.

Doug Terranova, he'll bring the tigers in and let them play and watch them. This one likes to stand on his hind legs, say, and another one might be a little wobbly. So he'll teach the one who likes it to do that trick. Almost every trick that an animal does is a natural thing that they do in the wild. They stand on their hind legs in the wild. Some of them do it better than others. Even like walking up the high wire, there's times they do that. There's no magic to it, it's just hard work.

• • • • •

Sharon: Do you ever travel with the show?

John: No.

Tom: We decided we want to get people to come there to see the museum and the grounds.

Sharon: Your season starts when?

John: June the twenty-fourth, and it goes through Labor Day.

Sharon: Every weekend?

John: Oh, it's every day. Seven days a week.

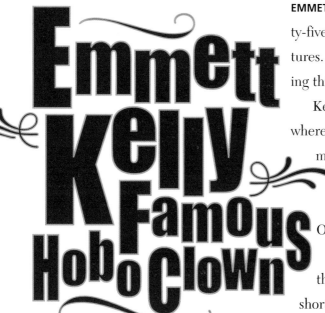

Emmett Kelly Famous Hobo Clown

EMMETT KELLY BEGAN LIFE IN KANSAS AS THE CHILD OF A FARMER. AS A TEENAGER HE TOOK A TWENty-five-dollar correspondence course and got a job at the Adfilm Company, drawing caricatures. He first drew his famous hobo cartoon in 1920 for a bread advertisement. It was during this job that he met Walt Disney, also a beginning cartoonist.

Kelly's first entertainment job was with Doc Grubb's Western Show Property Exchange, where he painted carnival Kewpie faces for six cents apiece. When he'd saved enough money, he bought a trapeze rigging and joined Zieger's United Shows and Frisco Exhibition Shows but was allowed only to paint carousels and sell tickets. Finally, he began touring in small circuses as a trapeze artist. This went on for nine years. Occasionally he would shift jobs and work as a whiteface clown.

Kelly introduced the Weary Willie clown character in 1932. During the winter of that year, he was touring nightclubs with a "chalk-talk" act, sketching scenery for the short skits he performed and drawing comic pictures for the audience. He came dressed in the Weary Willie costume.

As the 1932 season began, he toured with Otto Griebling on the Hagenbeck-Wallace Circus as a whiteface clown, and his hobo character, now well developed, made its circus debut that year. John Ringling North saw Kelly's Weary Willie at the Bertram Mills Olympia Circus in London in 1942 and invited him to join the Ringling Brothers and Barnum and Bailey Circus.

Emmett Kelly was the first modern clown who was allowed to stay in the ring while others performed. Both the Cristiani and the Wallenda troupes, headline aerial acts for Ringling, found that Weary Willie added an effective comic contrast to the drama of their performance.

Kelly appeared in several Broadway shows and films during the 1950s. Many of them featured his most famous skit, where he tries to sweep up the spotlight in the center ring. A personality in itself, the spotlight eludes him, and Weary Willie follows it with his broom. Kelly varied the details: sometimes the spotlight would blow up to full size when Willie sneezed; sometimes he ended the skit by sweeping the spotlight under a rug; in other variations it followed him out of the ring or shrank smaller and smaller until it faded altogether. In the 1970s Kelly did the skit on the *Carol Burnett Show*, sweeping the spotlight into the dustpan of Burnett's cleaning lady character.

Tom Dunwoody, the director of the International Circus Hall of Fame in Peru, Indiana, tells the following story:

Emmett Kelly and Walt Disney started together in St. Louis and Kansas City. They were street artists. Kelly was a bum, and so was Walt Disney. They went to Kansas City, and they did caricatures for a living. I guess Walt went out to Los Angeles and got involved in cartooning and animation, and Emmett came to Peru. The only reason the circus kept him around is because he could paint wagon wheels. I don't know where he learned it, but I'm sure there are old-timers around here who could tell you about it, because the painting style goes back a couple hundred years. They pass it on to each other.

You can't do acrobatics or aerial work for very long; when you turn thirty, you've got to do something else. Emmett became a whitefaced clown, just like the other fifty clowns on the Hagenbeck-Wallace circuit. He had been drawing this caricature, which he called Weary Willie. Basically, he was drawing himself before he joined the circus, and he decided to try the idea as a clown character. Then Otto Griebling, who developed the whole "tramp clown" idea in the first place, taught him all the techniques, the mime, all the funny moves.

He went over to England with the Bertram Mills Circus and the queen happened to be there, and she just thought he was great. It made all the papers. All of a sudden, Kelly, who had gone over there as a nobody, came back as a famous clown.

Gilbert Taylor

Interviewed by Sharon L. Smith
29 March 2000

Gilbert Taylor is the curator of the Crispus Attucks Museum in Indianapolis. Gilbert's father, Hugh Taylor, was a trombonist who played in a minstrel band in the Sells-Floto and Hagenbeck-Wallace Circuses in the 1920s. Although many circus performers wintered in Peru, Taylor lived with his family in Indianapolis during the off months, joining the circus when it came into Indianapolis and traveling with it for the season.

• • • • •

Gilbert: I'll talk about the vivid memories I have. I guess the most prominent thing is when my father would travel with the circus, and they'd travel south. He could talk about some of the horror stories that he experienced in the South. None of our family members could travel south—in fact, I didn't travel south until I was an adult—because he really forbade us going. He would talk about how he would go into some of the towns and the train would take off and he'd have to run to catch up with the train

It was very exciting to have someone in the family who was with the Circus.

to get on, and how they were treated separately and differently. Those were some of the hard times he had.

Some of the fun times, of course, were when they would come and visit at our home and have a big picnic, and we'd have an opportunity to talk with the entertainers. Of course they didn't have any of their animals and you didn't really know who they were because they just dressed regularly. And then to go and visit with them on site at the circus, and to see them with the animals and so forth, and to have lunch with them, which was a really big thing because they would always come over and kind of pick on our family. And to see the circus unload from the train and to walk to the site where they would entertain. And then of course the opening night, which was always a big, big thing. We would go maybe two or three times when the circus was playing. The entertainers became like friends and family members, and during the entertainment we could say, "There's so-and-so!" and wave at them. So it was a very exciting experience that way.

It was very exciting to have someone in the family who was with the circus. I can't remember any other friends or any other person that I knew whose family member participated in the circus. So many times I would say that, and people would just not believe that I had a family member who participated in the circus.

I know that my father was concerned about our family when he was on the road and tried to spend as much time at home as possible. He would tell many interesting stories about his travel and the fun experiences he would have.

Sharon: Did they treat black people differently in the circus?

Gilbert: The circus did not. Most of the sideshow people from what I understood kind of hung together. They were both black and white in the sideshow and, of course, my father was a musician, so he was even different than many of them, but there was no bias, as I understood it, in the circus in terms of race itself. It was the townspeople in the places they went.

• • • • •

Sharon: Did they walk the circus through Indianapolis?

Gilbert: The train would unload, I remember it being somewhere around English Avenue, and they would walk from the train to the site. They didn't go through downtown, but they went through the city. People would be lining the way as they walked.

Sharon: It was quite a big day, I take it.

Gilbert: Right. Good advertisement for the circus. They performed in a big vacant lot on Southeastern [Avenue], where Montgomery Ward is now.

I can remember the sideshow tent because everybody had their gold stage area, and you'd go from one platform to the other. There'd be the snake lady and the giant.

There were separate tents—you had to go out of one to get to the other ones. The big top was where you had the elephants and the tigers and the trapeze artists. The animals were all kept in one tent, and they were in cages and you could go in and see them. I remember monkeys, and I remember tigers and elephants and the giraffes. I remember them getting water for them—they had to be close to a water source to get water for the animals. And the feeding—I can remember they would stack up hay for them, not just to eat but they put it in the cage, too.

• • • • •

Sharon: Your father left the circus when either your sister or your brother was born, you said?

Gilbert: Right. I remember them talking about him coming off the road because he wanted to be with the family. And also, he wanted to perform at the Walker Building. . . . They had silent pictures there, and they'd have musical background and the organ and all. Then when they introduced talking movies they knocked him out of business.

Sharon: But he got jobs elsewhere?

Gilbert: Oh, yes. He played with Dudley Storms, he played with Leo Hines, he played all up and down the Avenue [Indiana Avenue]. He played the Columbia Club on the Circle, and many of those local places. He didn't have to suffer in terms of music at all. I remember during World War II when things were rationed, we had a big fifty-gallon drum that we buried in the ground in our backyard so that he would have enough gas so that he could go and play at various places. He would siphon the gas when he needed more and didn't have the ration stamps to get it. Those were interesting, fun times, and we didn't think they were so hard at the time. We grew gardens, and my mother—she could take a penny and she could stretch it to no end.

Harry Dawson

KENTUCKY-BORN GOVERNOR GREENUP DAWSON, OR Harry, owned, managed, and performed in a medicine show that was headquartered in Indianapolis beginning in 1905. Dawson wrote and sang his own songs and did a blackface comedy routine accompanied by his wife Carrie and his brother Lum. When his brother and his wife passed away, he remarried and continued to travel with his brother Leon.

Dawson's medicine company was called the Iceland Medicine Company, which accepted orders through the mail. He traveled and performed as the Dawson Concert Company. In addition to musical and comedy acts, the show featured clowns, midgets, contortionists, jugglers, and high-wire performers. Every summer Dawson, his family, and several hired performers would go on the road, posting broadsides around the neighborhoods and luring children to the show by meeting them in front of the performance venue—usually the opera house—to throw coins at them.

Dawson referred to his artists as "high class Vaudeville Entertainers" and reassured small-town parents with advertising that described his show as "All Star Artists, All Feature Acts, All Ladies and Gentlemen," "An Act that Merits the Approval of Any Audience," and "Everything Clean and Refined."

The Indiana Historical Society library holds the Governor Greenup Dawson Collection (M333, BV 1893–94).

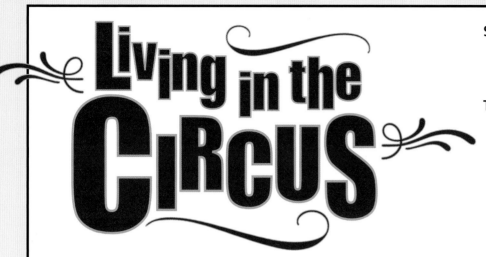

Living in the Circus

**From Tom Dunwoody interview
with Sharon L. Smith
2 February 2000**

Tom Dunwoody is a retired architect with an abiding love for the circus. He took on the directorship of the International Circus Hall of Fame in Peru in the early 1990s.

• • • • •

Tom: I had one old-time circus guy tell me about his life here during the season, when everyone else was on the show. He didn't go out one year, he stayed here, and basically he took care of the animals. They always had a few extra animals because they had a huge collection of wildlife. They may have had a couple of elephants that were crippled or were sick that they didn't take out and maybe some lions and tigers, and he'd take care of them. He was a forge worker during the winter, he fixed wagons and shod the horses.

Sharon: What kind of pay are we talking about?

Tom: Very little, very little. They still don't pay a lot in the circus. He told me they paid him $4.75 a week as an elephant tender. This was in 1937.

Sharon: That's during the depression. I guess that's not bad.

Tom: They got three meals a day and a place to sleep. It wasn't all that great a place to sleep—he said the bedbugs were so bad, he always went out and slept on the flatcars, even if it was raining.

Sharon: I'm not sure I would want to do that! But I understand that people who have been in the circus long enough didn't want to do anything else.

Tom: It gets in your blood. They say you "get sawdust in your veins." Living on that train—now today it's not too bad, because they all have their own campers and RVs. In the old days all they had was a trunk to call their own. The trunk was carried in the wagon, so they had to get from the train to that pad room [a dressing room behind the big top] in their civilian clothes to find their trunk.

Everything they carried was in that trunk—their costumes, their makeup, their memorabilia. They had four-foot-by-four-foot space—a trunk and two buckets of cold water—and that was their home. They took their bath right there, and they dressed right there in front of everybody. A few years ago Mena Ball put on a demonstration of how they used to bathe. She had a bathrobe, and she did the top part and then the bottom part and then the middle part, without exposing anything.

• • • • •

Tom: Back in the old days married people couldn't even sleep together. They had women's sleeping cars and men's sleeping cars.

Sharon: How did anybody have children if husband and wife couldn't sleep together?

Tom: Well, they never had a show on Sunday. So Saturday they'd go to town and they'd have a day off. That was wash day. Everybody would get a hotel room for Saturday night and maybe even Sunday night if they played that town on Monday. This was a big deal to them. But the circus had real strict rules. You couldn't fraternize with the workingmen. If two people fell in love, they couldn't get married, they just got fired.

Sharon: Why?

Tom: Apparently they didn't want the trouble. If they got married they'd want to sleep together and the way the circus was run on the railroad, you couldn't have that.

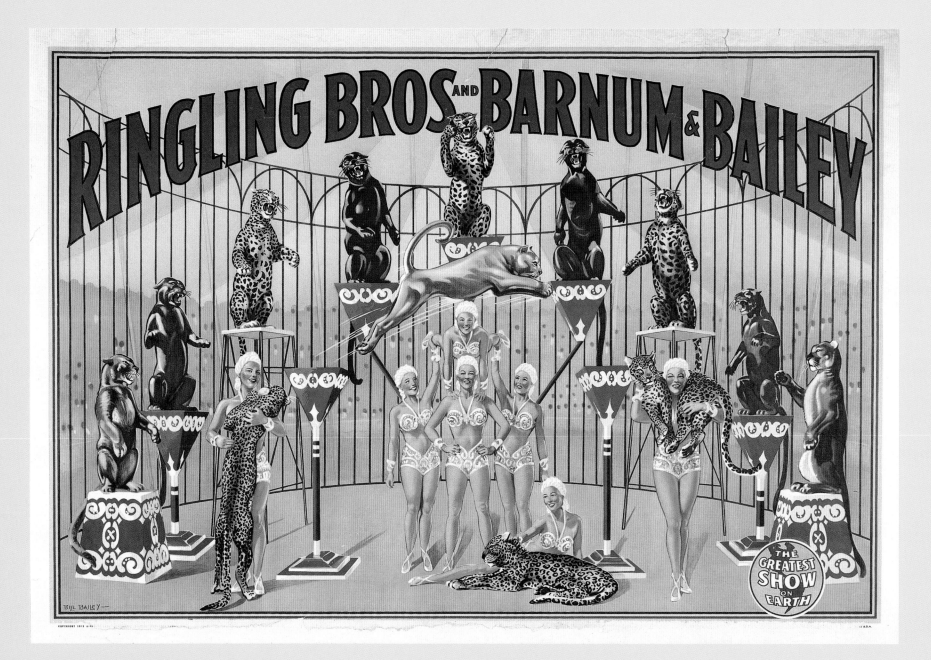

Joyce & Homer Ferguson

**Interviewed by Sharon L. Smith,
with John Fugate**

23 February 2000

Joyce Ferguson is the daughter of Clyde Beatty, who was a world-famous animal trainer. Born and raised in Peru, Joyce has been married to Homer Ferguson for fifty-five years, and their children and grandchildren are all avid circus fans. Joyce's daughter, granddaughter, and grandson have performed in the Circus City Festival for several years, and Joyce serves on the board of directors of both the Circus City Festival and the International Circus Hall of Fame.

• • • • •

Sharon: Tell me about your father.

Joyce: My dad was a wild-animal trainer. He was born in Bainbridge, Ohio. When he got out of school, he decided to join the circus. My grandma said he always was having kids over, and they were putting on circus acts and things when they were real young. But that [cat training] was something that caught his eye, and so he came here to Peru.

Sharon: When was that?

A lot of cat trainers would work with tigers, or they did lions. He was the first to put them together and survive. It was very scary.

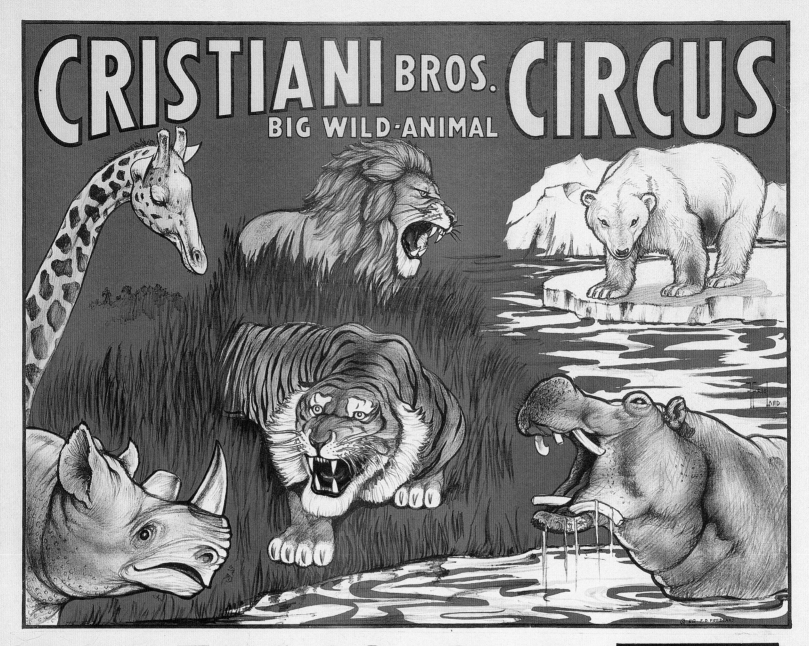

Joyce: He was eighteen, so about 1921 or 1922.

John: He started as a cage boy out at the winter quarters.

Joyce: Yeah. And then they've got pictures of him where he had trained a hippo, and he would take that around the hippodrome track for the spec [the "spectacle," a parade that takes place just before intermission].

John: You had three rings in a three-ring circus. And if you look at it there's an oval track around the three rings. You walk in on that track to find your seat. And it's referred to as the hippodrome track. That's where the spec goes, it's where all the horses go, it's where all the riding is done.

Joyce: He trained the hippo, and then he got into bears—trained big brown bears. At one time on the Hagenbeck-Wallace show, he had two acts for one show. The first one had pumas and llamas and a lion or a tiger, and the second act was nineteen tigers. . . . He started wanting to train lions and tigers so bad, and I think he started out with probably about nineteen, and then he gradually added until he had over forty in the cage at one time. Which was very rare.

Sharon: Who taught him? Was there anybody in particular that he trained under?

Joyce: There was a fellow on the Hagenbeck-Wallace show, and he worked with Dad, and I can't recall his name right now [Jules Castane].

John: He was kind of in the twilight of his career.

Joyce: Yeah, he retired, and Dad took over the act.

John: Most animal performers work that way. They take him in as a protégé and develop his act from there.

Sharon: That seems to be the way it works across the board.

John: In just about any act, but especially wild-animal

acts. You can't just walk in one day—you could be an acrobat and be in good physical shape and not be in the circus, but you can't get exposure to the animals, even in a zoo, like you do working with exotic animals in a show, day in and day out, traveling.

• • • • •

Joyce: We had our big circus winter quarters out here where the Circus Hall of Fame is. That's where he would go and they'd work on their act to get it ready to go out on the road. Boy, what a day; on the weekend that was fantastic. They'd be lined up in cars to get out there to see all of the performers practicing their act. That was about the most exciting thing there was to do.

Sharon: Did you live here?

Joyce: Yeah, we lived down Main Street. He was good with us kids. I think I had the first aluminum bicycle that was out that he bought. He bought me a white fur coat every year until high school, and I've still got that one upstairs in the cedar chest. Of course, he loved white. He dressed in white to perform.

Sharon: So did you train under him?

Joyce: No. I did not perform. I would go during the summer months and ride elephants or horses in the spec and just have fun. Usually took a high school girlfriend or something.

• • • • •

Sharon: Can you run through a day for him?

Joyce: The cats would be shipped in cars and usually he would get there pretty early on the grounds and watch them put up the tent and watch them get everything set up, and he always had a real nice trailer that he stayed in, and so he'd stay there until it was time for the show to begin.

Sharon: Did he go on the railroad with people, or did he drive in his own trailer?

Joyce: He was on the railroad circus, and then he went to the trailers and driving.

Sharon: How did he train his cats? How did he get them to do what he wanted?

Joyce: Out at the circus winter quarters, he would get them out of the cage, and they would be pretty grown up—they're not little—and there's a way that they would tie them with ropes, so the cat wouldn't jump and hurt itself. And then he would just go through the actions of saying and telling it what it has to do. Usually you had another cat that would do it, and the new one would learn it from that.

He never hurt the cats. He carried a gun that had blanks in it; he carried a whip to make them sit down, and he carried a chair. I've got a couple of those chairs out here that are just bit up, you know, with all these teeth marks. That's all he used. He had a guy who stood outside the cage, and if he needed any help or anything, he'd shove in a stick or a pole or something, if he had to get them away from him. I don't think Dad ever had that much trouble.

Homer: When he'd get through with his act, he'd be wringing wet from top to bottom. He'd always have a highball when he got through.

Joyce: He'd put on a white robe and he'd take his drink and go out and talk to all the lions and tigers. He wanted to tell them about their performance, and then he'd settle down and cool off, then he'd come in and he was fine.

Sharon: Did he talk to them often when he was training them?

Joyce: He did two or three shows a day, and he would do the same thing after every show.

Sharon: So they've got this focus on him, they know who he is, and they know what they're supposed to do.

Joyce: Oh, yeah, he could walk into a building—

Homer: And they'd start growling—

Joyce: Every one of them just stood up and walked back and forth and growled and growled because they knew it was him.

Sharon: I wonder how they knew? By the shape of his head or the sound of his voice—

John: Or the smell. They have a very pronounced olfactory sense.

Joyce: I thought that was neat. I'd go in there with him, and they'd all stand up and start prancing, looking at him, and everything.

• • • • •

Joyce: When the animals would come in[to the cage in the center ring], his top leader was Nero the lion, and he would go up first and get on the pedestal, and then the other two, and they just knew.

• • • • •

Sharon: So he had lions and tigers—

Joyce: Lions and tigers, over forty. In the early times he had black panthers, and he had leopards in the cage.

John: One thing I'd like to interject here, and you're probably missing it, is that a lot of cat trainers would work with tigers, or they did lions. He was the first to put them together and survive. It was very scary—

Joyce: Yeah, because they would fight each other.

John: There was that movie, *Ring of Fear*, which is basically the story of Beatty putting them together. He's talking to the circus owner, and he says, "When are you

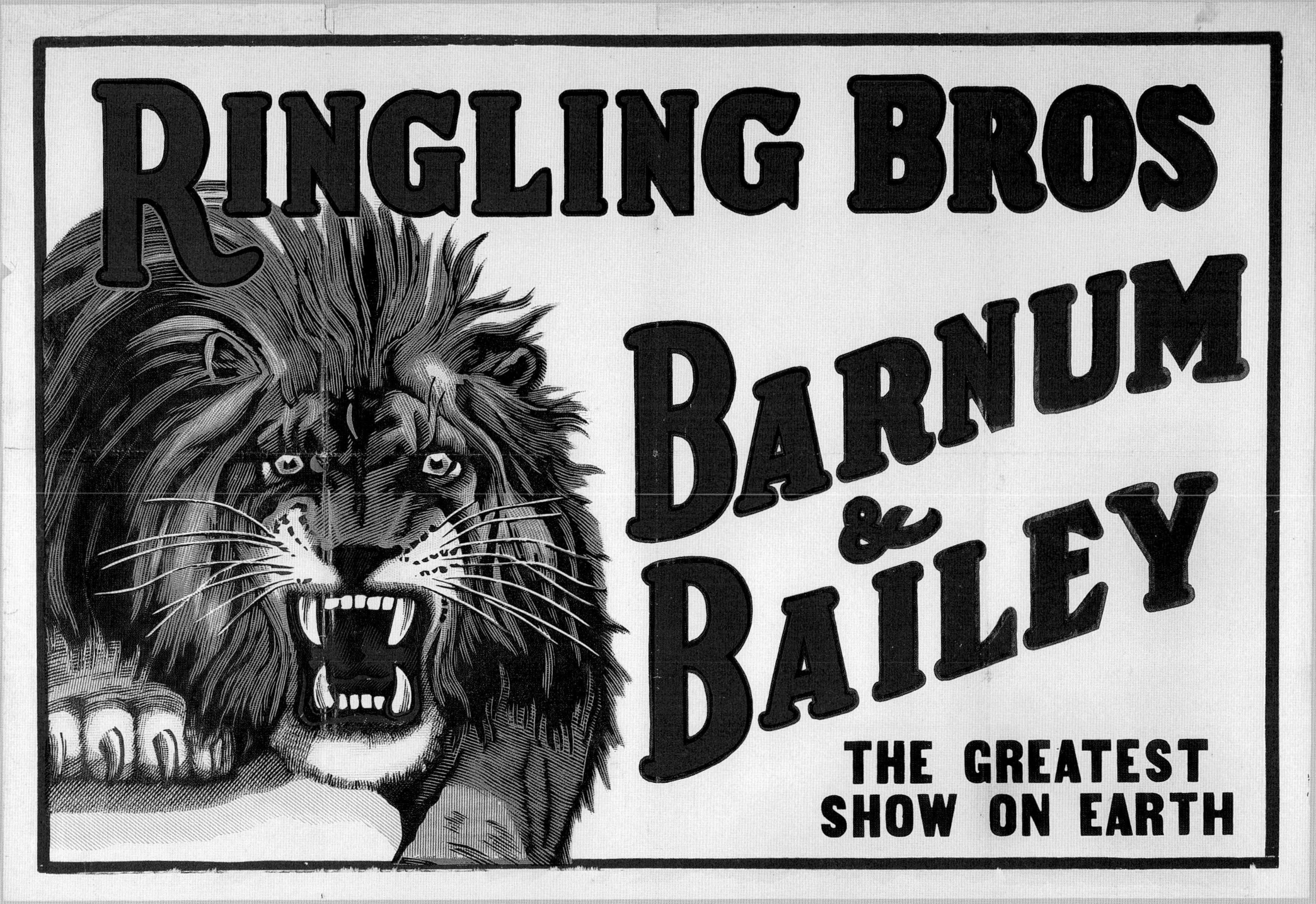
RINGLING BROS
BARNUM
&
BAILEY
THE GREATEST
SHOW ON EARTH

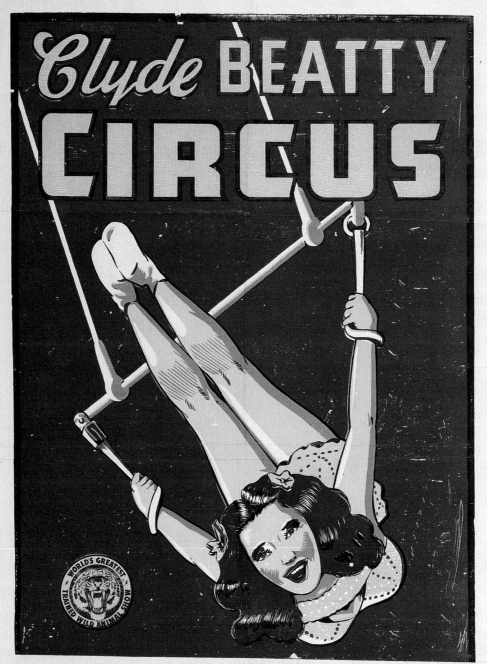

COLISEUM PARKING LOT VERMONT AVE. at 39th St.
LOS ANGELES

12 DAYS STARTS
WED. MAR.

FINAL PERFORMANCE SUN. NITE APRIL 1

going to mingle them?" Clyde says, "Tomorrow morning." The owner says, "Are you going to put a couple in?" Clyde says, "No, I'm putting all twenty of them in." And the guy looked at him like he was crazy. And he really only had one terrible fight between a lion and tiger, but they caught it on film.

● ● ● ● ●

Homer: Most of the circus people, just like the hands, they never got paid full salary. They only gave them half their salary, and when they got through at the end of the shows and went to winter quarters, then they'd give the other half because they'd all get drunk and leave the show. That was the way they held onto them.

Sharon: That's a piece of information I'd not ever heard before. They didn't get paid much!

Homer: They'd feed 'em good.

Sharon: Yeah, room and board, and in the 1930s that was worth a lot.

Joyce: You know, out here it was just like a little city. They had their own power plant, their own fire chief, it was just like a little city.

Homer: They still had the barns and everything out there [when he was fire chief], and we used to go out there once in a while with a truck—and I think it's still there—they had a standpipe come up, and it went down and out into the river. They would draw the water out of the river and feed the hydrants. We used to go up there and test the standpipe to make sure it was working. One standpipe's still there. The end of it's probably all closed up.

● ● ● ● ●

Joyce: My dad had his own zoo. He started a zoo in Fort Lauderdale, and that's what he was going to do during the winter months. He was so excited about it. But the city grew up around it and made him close it down. He looked out here—he was going to come out here and get Kelly's farm [across from Grissom Air Force Base, a farm that used to be a smaller, independent circus winter quarters]. He really wanted to start something like that where he could be more at home. Never got the chance. My dad died of cancer. He worked right up until probably eight or nine months before he died. He lived in Ventura, California.

John: He's buried where all the circus performers are buried, and all the famous actors? Forest Lawn?

Joyce: Yes. Sandy [her daughter] got on the Internet the other night and pulled up the grave he's buried in, and it's got a great big lion on that vault. It's really neat.

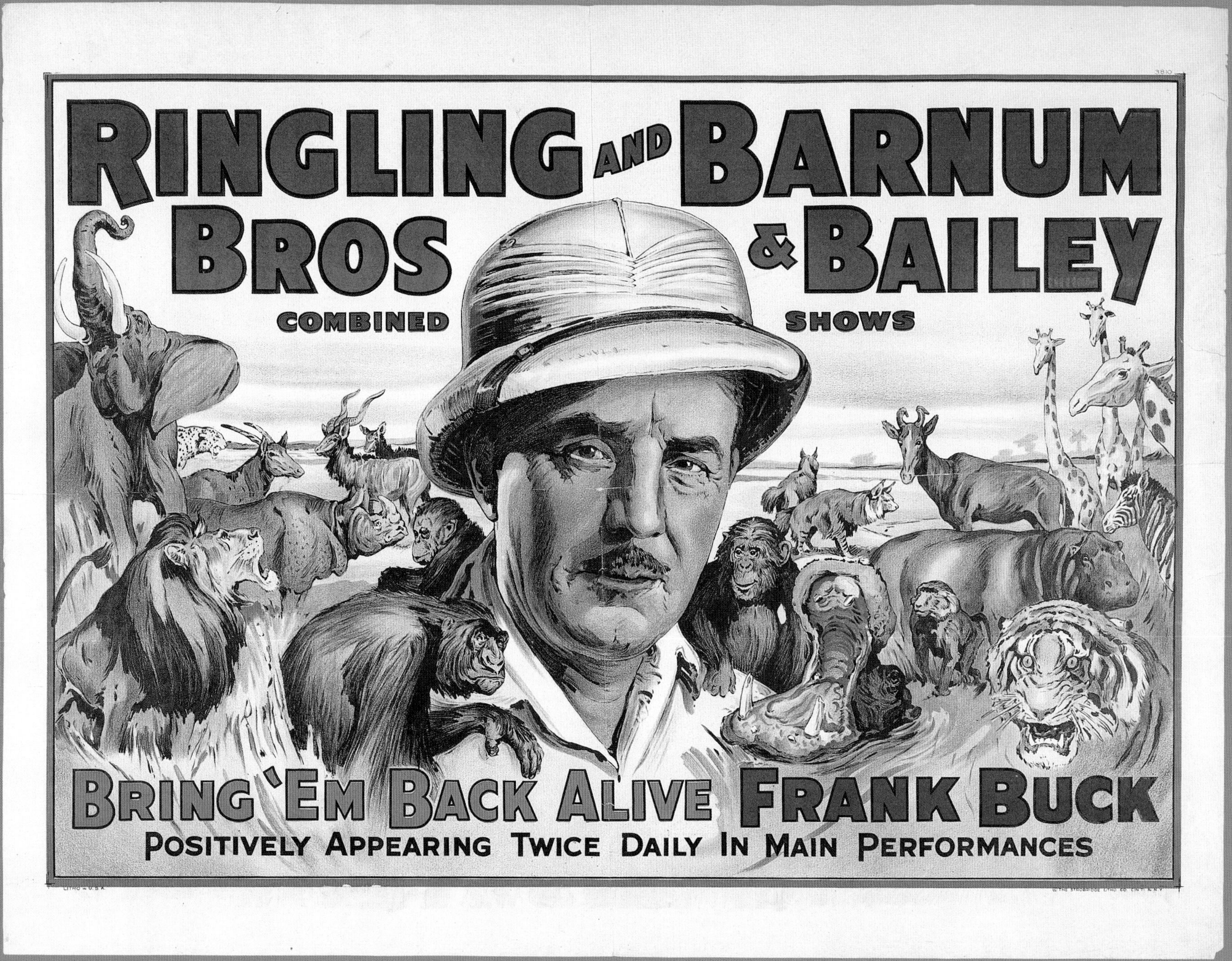
3810
RINGLING AND BARNUM
BROS & BAILEY
COMBINED SHOWS
BRING 'EM BACK ALIVE FRANK BUCK
POSITIVELY APPEARING TWICE DAILY IN MAIN PERFORMANCES
LITHO IN U.S.A.
© THE STROBRIDGE LITHO. CO. CIN'TI. & N.Y.

A RINGLING BROTHERS BOOKING AGENT SAW GERMAN-BORN LILLIAN Leitzel's Roman rings act in South Bend, Indiana, in 1914 and immediately signed her on. For her vaudeville act she did a never-before-seen stunt, the "one-armed flange," for which she separated her shoulder joint again and again, throwing her entire body vertically over her shoulder. Four feet nine inches tall and ninety-five pounds, she performed her one-armed flanges fifty feet in the air, with only a thin rubber mat below her.

Leitzel made her circus debut in 1915 at the Chicago Coliseum and moved to the headline spot in 1917, pulling in huge audiences as the "Queen of the Air." Posters proclaimed that she was "The World's Most Marvelous Lady Gymnast." Dramatic, talented, and as beautiful as she was tiny, Leitzel commanded top billing longer than any other circus performer in history.

She played her center-ring role to the hilt. She had a fiery temper and was known to slap and curse at her roustabouts if they didn't do her rigging just right. She traveled in her own private Pullman car, complete with a baby grand piano, and had a personal maid—who was repeatedly fired and rehired. Ringling Brothers paid her the then incredible salary of $1,000 a week.

In the mid-1920s Leitzel met Alfredo Codona, a Mexican trapeze artist with an equally fiery personality who had come to Ringling by way of a family circus and the Peru-based Hagenbeck-Wallace Circus. By the time they met, Codona was nearly as famous as Leitzel. He was billed as the "King of the Air," and his stunts began where other performers left off. He did the first triple somersaults in trapeze history as well as double pirouettes back to the bar, all with remarkable aerial height and elegance. His trademark swan-dive dismount was done headfirst and ended with what retired aerialist Mickey King calls a "twiddle of his feet," a scissor step done with pointed toes.

Codona and Leitzel fell madly in love and carried on a steamy courtship that was marked by screaming matches, breakups, and passionate reconciliations. Making it clear that she was running this partnership, Leitzel kept Codona waiting three hours at the altar when they married in 1928. Whatever quarrels the public might have witnessed, however, Codona was fiercely protective of Leitzel. When he wasn't performing himself, he would dress as a roustabout and stand under her rigging as she performed so that he could break her fall if he needed to.

The passionate, highly publicized marriage lasted three years. Constantly on the road, the couple went to Europe for engagements during the Ringling Brothers 1931 winter break, with Leitzel performing in Copenhagen while Codona performed at the Winter Gardens in Berlin. On 13 February Leitzel's swivel broke as she was doing her one-armed flanges. She fell to the cement floor, concussing her skull and injuring her spine. Two days later she died.

Codona was heartbroken and became reckless in his trapeze act. Although he married his partner, trapeze artist Vera Bruce, the marriage was unhappy. Codona's downward spiral accelerated when doctors grounded him after he tore the ligaments in his shoulder. Without his work to sustain him, Codona became desperate. In 1937, as he and Bruce were working out the details of their divorce in a lawyer's office, Codona shot and killed his wife, then turned the gun on himself.

As dramatic in death as he had been in life, in his suicide note Codona wrote, "I have no home, I have no wife to love me, I am going back to Leitzel, the only woman who ever loved me."

The Golden Age Romance of Lillian Leitzel & Alfredo Codona

Mena Ball

Interviewed by Sharon L. Smith, with Tom Dunwoody, John Fugate, Mickey King, and Pat Kelly

24 February 2000

Circus acrobat Mena Ball was born Melvina DeLong in Ohio in 1912. She and her two sisters formed an acrobatic act when they were children. They became known as the DeLong Sisters, and in 1927 John Ringling "picked them up," hiring them to travel and perform with the circus.

· · · · ·

Mena: This is about our beginning out in Ohio and then about how mother married this man—after her husband died—she married this fellow from Michigan, and he knew gymnastics, because he had run away from home when he was a boy and joined the circus. So he showed Gussie—she was the puny one in the family. The doctor told mother, "She's puny, gotta get her a bunch of exercise."

So he showed Gussie how to do bends and hand balances and jumps and things. That looked like a lot of fun, so Millie and I got into it. Before Millie was six, Gussie was ten, we were doing talent shows for the PTA.

…it's like a family. It is a family! Better than some families.

Nineteen twenty-three, on the showboat, the *Sunny South Showboat* on the Monongahela River and the other three or four rivers around there, we got booked on it. We sold these [promotional] postcards for ten cents apiece. We didn't even know how to make change at that age. Here we are, doing the tricks, you see. There was somebody else with our last name, DeLong, so we took Grandma's name, Scory. We were the Scory Sisters.

Sharon: Your dad was an acrobat?

Mena: Yeah, he did some acrobatics. He saw the performers, and so he learned it too. So he knew. 'Course, he left after a few years and became a mailman.

This scout happened to see us in Michigan, in Muskegon, where we were living, after playing the PTAs. This scout saw us, and he needed a free act for the outdoor show that was playing Muskegon, and the free act left the show, so he asked my dad—he knew about us because some of the Rotarians or the Shriners told him, "Hey, we got an act you can use!"—so we got booked. That was in 1922. In 1923 we were on a showboat. That was wonderful.

Nineteen twenty-five and 1926 we were on the Al Terrell main circus. In 1927 we were doing the Florida fair, and Ringling saw us, picked us up.

Sharon: What years were you with Ringling?

Mena: Nineteen twenty-eight to 1929, 1930, 1931, and we decided we'd get off in 1932 and go see the world. We didn't like it, so in 1933 we decided we wanted to come back. And Mr. Pat Valda, he says, "Oh, gee, girls, we're all booked up on the road, but you can have the [Madison Square] Garden." That was for four or six weeks. . . . John Ringling saw us work in 1927 at the Tampa, Florida, fair, and he come over to me and says,

"Would you like to work on the Ringling Brothers Circus?"

We was working on our act at that time. So we said, "Of course!"

But then Mr. Ringling says, "Mr. DeLong, we don't want you in the act, just the three girls. They'll be more attractive to the audience. You can be a clown."

Sharon: What did your dad think of that?

Mena: Well, we got three salaries! And Mom was the wardrobe lady.

• • • • •

Sharon: So you were a family on the road, then.

Mena: Yes.

Sharon: How did that work? When you're on the road, you're in trains. Did the family all stay together?

Mena: Oh, yeah, we all stayed together. We had either four or five bunks—I think we had four bunks. I never did know how Mom and Dad slept together in the same bunk.

Sharon: That'd be crowded, wouldn't it?

Mena: That's what I always thought!

Sharon: I guess you'd get used to it.

Mena: I don't know [about how her parents slept in one bunk], I'll have to ask one of my sisters. Anyway, we had two sections, two bunks on one side and two bunks on the other side of the car. And then we always walked to the lot together, and we walked home together, we ate our meals together. Heck, we were more of a family than people who lived in town.

• • • • •

Sharon: It must have been pretty hard to get educated, if you were a little kid.

Mena: Mom wanted us to learn violin. We had been prac-

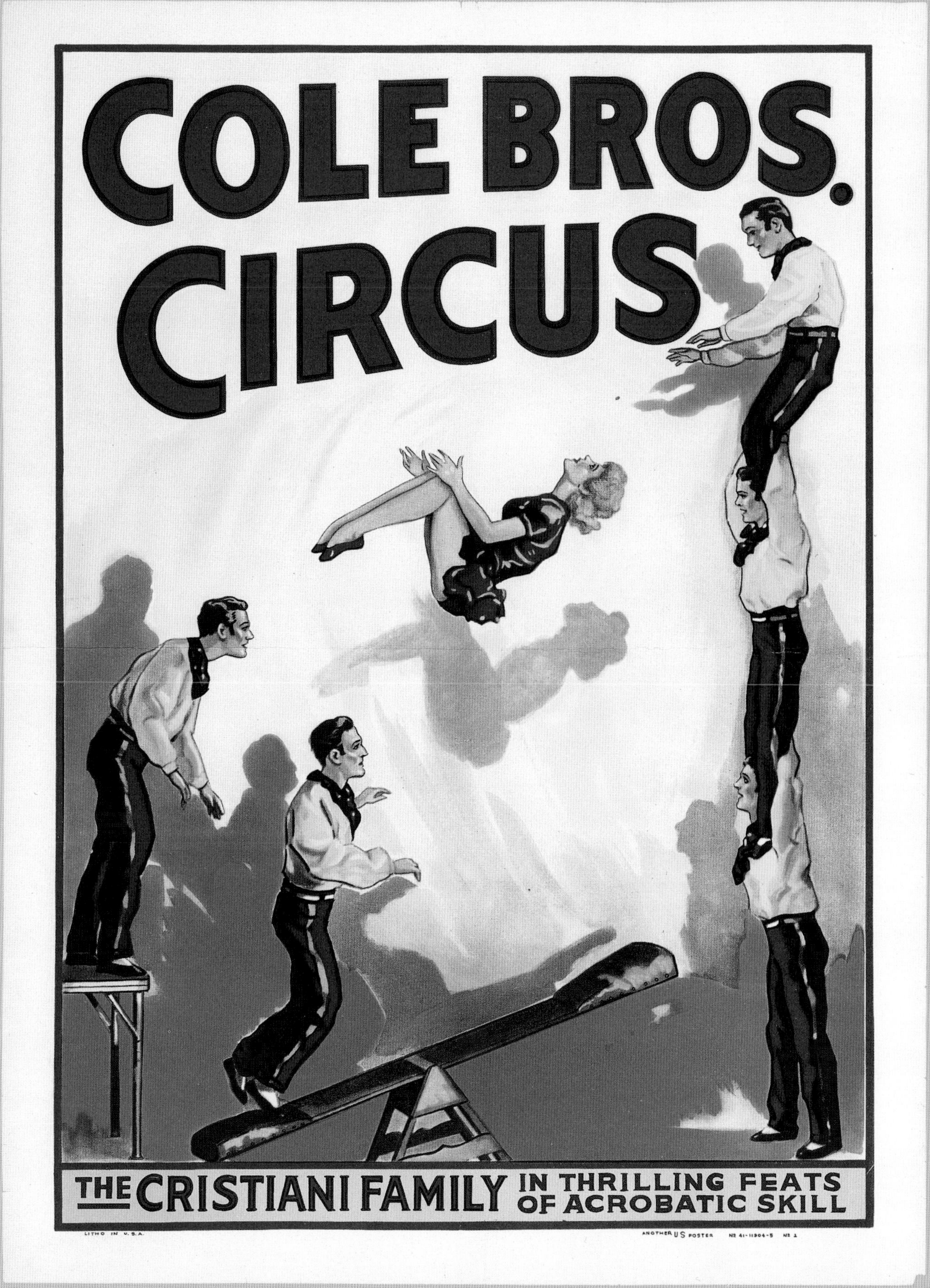
COLE BROS.
CIRCUS
THE CRISTIANI FAMILY IN THRILLING FEATS OF ACROBATIC SKILL
LITHO IN U.S.A.
ANOTHER US POSTER Nº 41-11904-5 Nº 1

ticing violin in vaudeville, you know. Palidor, the Italian clown, he was a violinist clown. Mom asked him if he'd teach us—Gussie and I—give us lessons on the circus. He said, "Yeah, sure, sure," so one day we got our violins, and he and the two of us walked around behind a wagon—oh, about a hundred feet away—we practiced. Then we come back to Mom in the dressing room, and she said, "Girls, I don't think we have to practice violin anymore this summer; we'll do it in the wintertime." They heard us practice.

Sharon: [Laughing.] Violin is so hard. It's hard to play well.

Mena: Squeak, squeak, squeak! I think there was some remarks made. We never will forget that. We liked it.

Sharon: So there was a clown who played the violin in his act, or did he just play the violin?

Mena: I don't know if he ever played it in the act, but he was a violinist. He always had his violin with him. Same as the Wallendas, you know, they were a musical family, too. [The Wallendas are a famous Italian high-wire act, several generations strong, who are still active in the circus. This particular generation of Wallendas did a seven-person pyramid, performing forty feet in the air without a net. They worked with Ringling from 1927 to 1946.] Nobody knows that. They gave us a Victrola.

See at night, we'd all go to the train, and the train wouldn't pull out for a couple hours, so we'd sit around and talk and drink our Coke or lemonade or whatever—maybe the men might have a beer, I don't know—and the Wallendas, we told him how nice it was to hear that music, and they said, "Well, we've got something you can play." It was a little Victrola that was made out of brass. It wasn't any higher than that [she describes it with her hands, and the dimensions are about six inches

cubed]. It looked like a large powder box. If you lifted the lid up, it had the arm, and it would play these regular-sized records. You could sit the little machine here, put that record on it.

· · · · ·

Sharon: Were you on the road when you were young enough to need schooling—math and English?

Mena: You learned it [English] from talking. We read a lot. Mom spoke broken English, you might say. Her family always spoke Belgian at home. She learned Italian by herself—her husband was Italian. Some of his friends were Hungarian, so my mother learned Italian, Hungarian, and Belgian—and English. We learned everything—I don't want to say the hard way, but that's what you'd say. We learned it through actual use.

Sharon: Actually, I think that's a better way to learn it.

Mena: Yes! At the age of fourteen I was teaching the acrobatic troupe's little girl—she was five—she translated English into Spanish for her mother. I had her to teach her her ABCs and her numbers. I've still got a sheet of paper where she was writing her alphabet.

Sharon: And you were teaching.

Mena: We each taught ourselves. Yeah. My younger sister only went to the fourth grade. I went clear to the fifth. That's when we started going on the road.

· · · · ·

Sharon: Tell me what a three high is.

Mena: I'm on the bottom, standing up. Then Gussie gets up on my shoulders—there's a way of getting up. Then Millie is facing me on the floor, she's got Gussie's hands, and they work together and Millie stands on my shoulders on Gussie's feet. Then Millie and Gussie get the handhold, and Millie swings up to the top of Gussie's shoulders.

That's the three high. So we did it at Madison Square Garden. That was about our most sensational trick, you know, for girls. But there was another troupe doing that.

Those [Ringling] performers were so nice, they did everything to make us shine. The Hungarian bareback riding family showed us how to do the bow, showed us style. They really put the polish on us. That's why we went to Europe.

Sharon: You performed in front of Hitler and his officers?

Mena: Yes. I have an idea why he did that. We were nice looking, we were athletic, and we looked darned healthy. We were Caucasian, too. No wonder he wanted to give him a private show. We were everything he liked! I have a souvenir of it, a ribbon that's twelve inches wide and three yards long. It's got gold words on it and the date: April 16, 1937, "With the Friendship of the German People." It came with a dozen roses. Each one of us got that. I've still got it; that's in my trunk.

We were there [in Hamburg] in 1938. Millie and I went over there to keep the apartment for my brother-in-law. Gussie had come over to have a little baby; she had married over there. He was a sea captain from Brazil. Millie and I went over from Indiana, I think it was July, and we stayed six months, until the end of the year.

Do you know we had to wait two weeks at the end of that year to get a ship to come back to the States? They were loaded with Americans getting out of Hamburg, Germany. Even with connections, him being a sea captain, you know—he was stationed right there in Hamburg. He had to really work hard to get us a room on that ship. . . . They got out in 1939. My other sister and I came back in January of 1939. That was third class, too.

John: And Hitler started when, in April? Invaded Poland?

Sharon: I think so. [Hitler invaded Poland in early September 1939.]

Mickey: Was it a tough ride on the ship?

Mena: No, it was okay. You know, the young Hitler boys—I call them the Boy Scouts—knocked out all the windows of the Jewish stores. There in Hamburg, where we were living for those six months, we would go down to the grocery store. One morning we went down there, and he [the grocer] was gone. His wife was working behind the counter. She said, "Yes, they came and got him last night."

We lived in pensions, like boardinghouses, and in the one we were in Hamburg, there was a maid who had hair down to the floor, and she was brushing it and brushing it in the washroom, and she said, "Please, when you go back, would you take me back with you? I will work five years for nothing if you will take me back with you. I am not getting married, I am not going to raise children for Hitler to put in a war." I'm telling you, those things get me.

• • • • •

Mena: [Looking at photographs.] In Sarasota, the Cannon Man, that's him right there. My stepfather, my mother, my older sister, my younger sister, and me. And this is Olga, his sister. We went over there for spaghetti and a bird supper.

Sharon: A bird supper?

Mena: Did you ever see a big platter, with little birds this high? Sparrows, robins, bluebirds, everything? That's what Zachini cooked for us. I mean to say it was delicious. All they did was take the feathers off and gut it and fried all the bones and everything—you have to—and—

John: Which Zachini fixed this for you?

Mena: Hugo. [Hugo Zachini is the man who shot himself out of a cannon, and Mena refers to him as the Cannon Man. He was the first to conceive of the modern form of the human cannonball and joined Ringling in 1929.]

We went back after we quit the circus—the second or third year after we left—and we visited everybody. We had quit, like that. We went back to visit the Ringling Brothers in Marion, I believe. That's my younger sister, she looks so pensive. This is one of the acrobats who knew her so well.

Sharon: When did you quit?

Mena: Nineteen thirty-eight. After my sister got married. That's the beginning.

Sharon: Which sister, Gussie?

Mena: Yeah. She's the one who married the sea captain. Merchant marine sea captain.

Sharon: She met him during the war?

Mena: No, he was stationed in Hamburg, Germany. We were performing in Hamburg, but he had met her on the ship. Nineteen thirty-six, going down to South America, we were on the same ship, and he said to the captain of that ship, "Please put the DeLongs at our table and introduce us all." His name was Hamlet. The mother named every kid after something in the opera.

That was in 1936. In 1937 we were playing Copenhagen, Denmark, and he came to Gussie and said, "This has gotta stop. We're going to get married."

Sharon: So he didn't want her to be in the show.

Mena: He had to go travel all the time by airplane to see her!

• • • • •

Mena: I haven't told you yet what we learned by being in the circus. We learned to accept people, no matter what color or country or language. Now remember, we were little children, we learned it from scratch. Even when they spoke different languages, we tried to learn what they were saying, and they tried to learn what we were saying. When you've been together for a long time, you cry when you say good-bye. Sing "Auld Lang Syne," and it brings tears to your eyes. The band plays it. A lot of people walked away without saying good-bye, it's too sad. When you meet each other in the spring, oh, is there a hugging contest. You see? We are a close bunch.

Sharon: Yes, you are; it's like a family.

Mena: It *is* a family! Better than some families. When you work together, you know better than to have any dissension in the ranks. That's your life. That's your living. You get along.

William Coup and the Circus Railroad Car

**From Tom Dunwoody interview
with Sharon L. Smith
2 February 2000**

IN **1872** WILLIAM COUP OF TERRE HAUTE, INDIANA, went to the mighty P. T. Barnum. He said, "Look, if we could put the circus on the railroad, then we could bypass all these small towns that are not profitable, we could go all the way from Cincinnati to Indianapolis overnight." See, they could only go ten miles a night in wagons, and they played every little town.

Barnum thought this was a good idea, and they went out and they hired some cars and they tried to load the wagons over the sides of the cars. It took them twelve hours to load the circus onto the train. Well, this wasn't going to work. It wouldn't work because when they rented out flatcars they were different heights, and a lot of them had the brake wheels in the way.

So they went to Columbus, Ohio, and they had a special train built. They had the brake wheels built clear down low. They made them all the same height, and they put little bridges between the cars. Then they put a ramp down at the end, so instead of running the wagons off the sides they just pulled them off the ends. The whole thing is continuous, it's one long ramp. They could do up to thirty flatcars, all hooked together. This completely revolutionized the circus. What I still find amazing is that the rest of the country didn't pick up on this until after World War II. They called it piggybacking, and it was invented by the circus in 1872.

The original circus train was just the short car, which would only hold two to three wagons on a flatcar, but after a while the circus doubled the length of the cars, from thirty-six feet to seventy-two feet long. They got charged by the car, so they could make them twice as long and still paid the same price. They still used the horses—the horses would pull the wagons over and down the ramps. The most dangerous job in the circus was not the lion tamer, it was the guy who had to guide that wagon down the ramp—if the wagons got loose, he'd be smashed.

Mickey King

**Transcript of a video produced
by the International Circus Hall of Fame,
John Fugate, interviewer**

6 August 1999

**And interview by Sharon L. Smith,
with Tom Dunwoody and John Fugate**

24 February 2000

Mickey King began her circus career in 1923 when she ran away from home and started traveling with the Peru-based Sells-Floto Circus. Trapeze artist and trainer Eddie Ward took her under his wing, and after his death she developed a solo act. She was famous for her one-armed flanges.

•••••

Tom: How did you get in the circus, Mickey?

Mickey: I ran away from home.

Sharon: Where's home?

Mickey: Holyoke, Massachusetts. We were living in Holyoke then.

Tom: I thought you were from Canada.

Mickey: Yes. But we migrated, honey. We migrated . . . down to Richford, Vermont, where my dad got a job. He took care of the boiler rooms and the furnace so they wouldn't explode. He had a wonderful reputation. From Richford we moved down to St. Albans. From there we moved to Sheldon Springs. That's where my little brother Clarence—the one that just got killed a couple

They are **Wonderful** people to be with. Not only as performers but **heart-to-heart people.**

years ago—was born.

Tom: How old were you when you ran away from home and joined the circus?

Mickey: I was eighteen. I ran away in July and turned nineteen August the sixth.

• • • • •

John: Mickey, when did you start in show business?

Mickey: Nineteen twenty-three.

John: And what circus was that?

Mickey: Sells-Floto. [Sells-Floto was one of the circuses that wintered in Peru.]

John: And you joined them on the road, right?

Mickey: Right. Greensville, Massachusetts. A town not far from Holyoke. We were living in Holyoke, and I ran away from home during the show in Greensville.

John: What's the first thing you did in show business?

Mickey: I stood underneath a swinging ladder and made my arms go to one side, and then the other, then sang a song, "Who's sorry now? Whose heart is aching?"

John: When did you start learning an act of your own?

Mickey: We weren't supposed to go in under the big top at any time, but I would take a peek between the side wall and the big top, just to see what they were doing, and when I saw all the things they were doing, I thought, "Well, gee whiz." I went downtown and bought two yards of material and made a little [outfit] for myself, and I went up the ladder, got into the flying trapeze catch trap [the trapeze rigging used by the catcher], and I was swinging back and forth, touching my toes to the canvas.

A gentleman came down the hippodrome track and he says, "Little girl, what are you doing up there?"

I says, "I'm swingin'."

He says, "Do you like it?"

I said, "Oh, I love it, yes."

He said, "Aren't you afraid to fall?"

I said, "No, no, I'm not afraid to fall."

He said, "Well, come down out of there." I crawled down the ladder and walked over to him. He said, "Who told you you could go up there?"

I said, "Nobody, but I saw everybody else swingin' in there. Do you own the circus, mister?"

He said, "No, I don't own the circus, but I own that rigging. If you want to get up there and practice and have fun, next time I put up the net I'll have the boys go over to you." Oh, I was in fool's paradise.

He said, "Go on back up there now, I want to see you."

So I went back up and got in the catch trap, and he come up the ladder. I hung by my knees, and he took a hold of my hands to see how much strength I had, and I budged him.

He said, "Do you want to be one of my girls?"

I said, "Oh, I'd like that, yes."

He said, "Well, when this show closes in the fall, you come with me to Bloomington, Illinois, and be one of my family." And that's what happened.

John: Who was this man?

Mickey: Eddie Ward of the Flying Wards.

John: So you went to Bloomington, Illinois, home of the flying trapeze, and you worked out of the famous barn there?

Mickey: Yes. I learned to hang by my knees and do swinging ladders, all the small tricks that everybody else can do, and pretty soon I was a flyer.

John: When did you start doing your own act?

Mickey: In 1929 Eddie Ward passed away. I loved him so much, I couldn't be around the show. I could hear him saying, "Come on, girls, get in step now, put your shoulders back," as we'd be walking in to do the flying act. I would get up the trapeze and they'd have the music, maybe "Over the Waves," and he'd say, "He knows how to play the right music for the flying act." After he passed away, I could hear that music. I loved him so much because he gave me my first start to make a way for myself in life.

So I had been practicing, trying to hang by one hand and all that sort of thing, and I was the only one that could do a straight back flange or a front flange. I had more strength and more technique. So I thought, "Well, by golly, I'm going to get away from here." From the Floto show, I left to go to Buffalo and practice. My mother was living in Buffalo, New York, and so I went to Buffalo and hired a theater. They weren't using it, so I paid them and I'd go in there and hang my rigging and practice. Antoinette [Mickey's sister, also an aerialist] got married [to Art Concello], and they made their own flying act. This was 1931 or 1932. They opened up in a little circus out west in Oklahoma City—there are so many of those little ones that I can't even remember the name—

John: The Russell Brothers Circus.

Mickey: Anyway.

John: How tall were you, and how much did you weigh?

Mickey: Four foot eleven and a half inches and I weighed a hundred pounds almost all of the time. "Skinny Minny," that's me.

• • • • •

John: Her costume was very risqué for her time. She was on the cutting edge. There, she's doing muscle grinds. [This is a technique where the performer holds onto the trapeze bar and flips over and over on his or her stom-ach.] People who do this today have a bar within a cylinder, so the bar turns. She didn't have that; she was grinding her skin away. The trapeze bar—the kind that turns—is called a "roller." [John's comments are a response to a film of Mickey performing in the 1930s.]

I've seen movies of your act, and I've been a friend of yours for a while now and got to know quite a bit about you. You've had a varied career. When did you start the one-armed flanges that made you famous?

Mickey: When I went to Buffalo and practiced in 1931. I went out to the show where Art and Antoinette were, and that was my first circus with one-armed swings. I had a terrible fall there, too.

John: Oh, really?

Mickey: Yeah. I was feeling pretty bad, and I told the manager of the show, I said, "I oughtn't go out and work tonight, I don't feel good."

He slapped me on the back and said, "Go on, Mickey, you work and you'll feel better." So I got up in the rings, and as I jumped out to catch by my knees, I went right straight out to the stage [face first]. They took me to the train and put me in Art and Antoinette's stateroom because I was out, and they knew if they took me to the hospital I wouldn't come to.

The next morning Antoinette was standing over me, wringing her hands, saying, "Mickey, Mickey, Mickey, Mickey, do you know me?" I looked up and said, "Sure I know you. I can tell you by your big green eye." All I could see was one of her eyes. So she started to go to pieces, and Art slapped her and said, "Stop it now. She's alright." From there on my next trip was Baltimore, Maryland, and I was black to my navel. So anyway. That's one fall.

John: How many times did you fall?

Mickey: Oh, my God. I fell in Cincinnati. I was doing a show with John Robinson for the Shrine. We had May Wirth [a famous equestrienne, or horse trainer], it was a big show, and the boys who put my rigging up put the pin in the shackle and didn't screw it in, so when I did the second show the screw worked out of the shackle and I fell to the stage. That's how I got this bad shoulder. It was four weeks before I could work.

The doctor would come and sit in the chair beside my bed to try and talk sense into me. I'd order a baked potato. "I wanna baked potato!" and they'd bring me this great big baked potato, and it'd get in the sheets—baked potato and butter—and I'd say, "Oh, there goes my waistline." And the doctor would said, "No way. Eat as much as you want; in fact, the more potato you eat, the better off you are."

• • • • •

Mickey: May Wirth and Frank Wirth, her husband, built a beautiful circus in Allentown, Pennsylvania, for about three weeks. They wanted a one-armed swinger, and I had been off about three weeks, deciding, "The heck with it," I was going to quit. They called me, asked me if I would come in and join the show, and they wanted to teach me to ride in May's place. I thought, "I hang by my teeth, do one-armed swings, swinging ladder, ride the horses, and I'm going to learn something else? No." So I sat down and I thought it over.

They called me back that night, and I said, "I've made up my mind that I will. I'll join you." When I got there, instead of teaching me to ride in May's place, they had someone else on their one-armed swings, and they wanted to ditch her. I was disgusted, but I thought to myself, "What can I do?" I said, "I got my one-armed

loop, but I haven't worked for so long, I probably won't be able to do ten." Frank said, "Mickey, I don't care if you do two. If you do two, you'll do two the next day, and the next day you'll do three. Don't worry about it."

John: What's the most you ever did at one time?

Mickey: Two hundred seventy-six is my record.

John: Where was that?

Mickey: In Springfield, Massachusetts, I was doing a show for the crippled children—a free show, ten o'clock one morning. I had a property boy—Jonesy was his name, Charlie Jones. I got to a hundred, and he said, "Mickey, my arms are getting tired." I just kept going, going, going, and I could hear the [Catholic] sisters saying to the kids—they had balloons, and they were going pop—and the sisters said, "Quiet now!" Two hundred seventy-six.

• • • • •

John: Did you ever work on the Cristiani Circus?

Mickey: I was with them the first show they did, in Detroit, Michigan. [The Cristianis date their circus origins back six generations, performing as bareback riders, acrobats, jugglers, and trapeze artists. They came to the United States in 1934 to perform with the Hagenbeck-Wallace show, by then owned by Ringling.]

Lucio and I fell in love with each other. [Lucio was one of twenty-four children—twelve sons and twelve daughters; he was one of the greatest bareback riders in history.] I got scared. I saw so many girls with so many boys, and they made a great big long table, and the boys had to sit down and eat first, the girls had to wait on them. I said, "Oh, Lord." That was the very first show they did when they come over [from Italy]. They are wonderful people to be with. Not only as performers but heart-to-heart people.

CEDAR FALLS

AFTERNOON & NIGHT

MON. JULY 16

CEDAR FALLS

AFTERNOON & NIGHT

MON. JULY 16

Pat Kelly

**Interviewed by Sharon L. Smith,
with John Fugate**

24 February 2000

World-famous circus clown Emmett Kelly had two sons, Emmett, Jr., and Pat. Both followed in their father's footsteps, creating their own hobo clown characters and traveling with the circus. With his mother an aerialist and his father a clown, Pat grew up in the circus. He lives in Peru, Indiana.

• • • • •

Pat: My mother used to say, "All those years I've been in the circus. I don't miss the circus, I miss the people."

• • • • •

Sharon: I just read a bunch of stuff about your dad [clown Emmett Kelly], but I wanted to know about you. There's a whole lot of stuff out there about your dad. [Long pause.] You have a scrapbook, don't you?

Pat: Oh, yeah. [Takes out scrapbook.] I was in the U.S. Marine Corps in 1953. This is 1954. I started [as a clown] in 1958 . . . from Peru. . . . Nineteen fifty-nine, I was with Adams Brothers Circus. Up in Wisconsin . . . canvas tent, not vinyl like nowadays. [The scrapbook contains clippings from newspapers in towns where he played. Some of them refer to circus performances, some of them refer to street celebrations, store openings, or store sales. Kelly's face is very expressive, and he talks with his hands; a lot of his con-

"All those years I've been in the circus. I don't miss the circus, I miss the people."

versation is about people and places he remembers.]

Sharon: You had a different costume from your dad—

Pat: Emmett, Jr., and I had to create our own. No, no, Dad wouldn't give us his costume. . . . I have two fathers. This is my stepfather, Joe Lewis, and he came from England.

Sharon: Your mom was in the circus, too, right?

Pat: She was a trapeze aerialist.

Sharon: Where'd she get her start?

Pat: Nineteen three. She learned trapeze when she was a little girl. Born in the circus. My father was from Kansas. Before she married my father, my mother was from Atlanta, Georgia. Eva Lewis. My mother and father, they did trapeze. When he started [in] the circus—he did trapeze.

• • • • •

Pat: Shriners have their own clown unit, and it's a union. Just the clowns.

John: All the Shrine circuses have their own clown units, so they kind of put the professional clown out of business.

Sharon: When did this all happen?

John: It started several years ago—late 1960s, 1970s—it has just kind of continued.

• • • • •

Pat: This is 1968, February to June. I'm property of George Hammond, eastern seaboard. My mother used to always say, "I'm property."

John: George Hammond Circus is still in business. It's producing a circus next weekend.

Pat: He was Mister Show Business, George Hammond. Nineteen sixty-one and 1968, he said, "Look around, because you're going to live here five months. If you have any complaints, you come to me." So he was Mister Show Business. George Hammond, God bless him.

• • • • •

Pat: Booking agent, booked me into Robbins Department Store for one month. I was stuck in a hotel there. I was living there, may as well just not come back to Peru. For one month. I hated like heck to come back to Peru because I got me a nice room, don't have to pull through a house trailer . . . only trouble is, my contracts ran out!

• • • • •

Pat: Here's my father.

Sharon: All this time, was your dad still working in the 1960s?

Pat: Oh, yeah, he was going strong.

Sharon: When did he officially retire?

Pat: He retired from Ringling, but he was still going, on TV and movies.

Sharon: Well, he got honored in 1973, according to this article.

• • • • •

Sharon: He was in movies—*The Fat Man*—

Pat: That's 1951. He was the lead star . . . with Rock Hudson, Jayne Meadows.

John: He was the killer. . . . He didn't want Weary Willie to become a killer, so he played it in whiteface. He was in *The Pied Piper*, too. In whiteface.

Sharon: So whenever he did a clown in a film, he'd do whiteface instead of his Weary Willie? [Emmett Kelly was in *The Greatest Show on Earth*, and he was in his Weary Willie persona, only once appearing out of costume and speaking a short line in the three-hour film.]

Pat: My mother did the "iron jaw" [in *The Greatest Show on Earth*, standing in] for Dorothy Lamour.

• • • • •

Sharon: So you don't talk when you're in costume, right?

Pat: No, no, no.

Ruby Haag Brown

**Interviewed by Sharon L. Smith,
with John Fugate and Tom Dunwoody**

22 March 2000

Ruby Haag Brown was born Ruby Fisher in Kentucky in 1911. Her father, a veterinarian, saw Mena Ball and her sisters perform in the circus as the DeLong Sisters and decided to teach his three daughters how to be circus performers. Ruby learned to do the "iron jaw," an aerial stunt in which she hung by her teeth in the air, and the "loop walk," where she "walked" across the wire trapeze rigging through a series of loops, forty feet in the air and upside down. The family act, the Fisher Circus, also included her mother's slack-wire performance and her father's trained ponies.

• • • • •

Sharon: Tell me the story about being in Alice the elephant's mouth.

Ruby: Well, she carried me in her mouth. She'd run down the track, they always announced it, you know, me in the elephant's mouth, and then she'd go down in front of the grandstands. All the way, you know, as long as there was a grandstand, she made that trip. Then she did another trick in the act, she held me by my knee, and I'd pose. She dropped me from that once, just one time, and I hit my back on the tub [that the elephants stand on], and I broke a rib. Kind of painful. She didn't mean to. I don't know what happened. Something probably scared her, and she opened her mouth. So I fell. That was at the stadium in Chicago.

John: A lot of people have done the leg carry that she's talking about, but she's the only person I've ever heard of who did that act.

Sharon: I take it that it didn't hurt you to be in her mouth?

Ruby: Oh, no, it didn't hurt a bit.

Sharon: Tell me, do elephants have teeth?

Ruby: Yeah, they do. About four inches long. Way back there. 'Course, I didn't touch her teeth, you know—

Sharon: So she had you in the front of her mouth?

Ruby: Yes. Of course, she had to have her trunk down to hold me. She didn't curl her trunk up or anything under me, she just went with me.

Sharon: How did you train her to do this?

Ruby: I didn't train her. My sister-in-law trained her. And then I did the trick. Helen [Haag] did it for a while, then, when I came back to the show, I did it.

• • • • •

Ruby: You know Harry James [the bandleader and trumpet player]? His mother was a contortionist on the show when we was on that show. He was born on the Haag show. His folks was with the Haag show.

John: He was actually named Harry Haag James.

Ruby: I've got a scrapbook, it's got a picture of him with his little drums.

[Ruby married Harry Haag, Jr., and she performed in his father's Great Haag Circus for several years, both as an aerialist and as an elephant trainer.]

Sharon: How did you meet Harry Haag?

Ruby: On the circus. He was a clown, but at that time they also called him the "fixer." He'd go to town and pay the license, and talk to the police, and you know, have everything ready for when the show came.

John: If something went wrong, he fixed it.

Ruby: Like a lawyer, or something like that.

[Ruby's sister Josephine also married a clown, Brownie Timberlake. Timberlake performed on horses, and sometimes he used Thai, a rhesus monkey from Thailand who liked to smoke cigarettes during the act. As she grew older, Ruby developed Ruby's Beauties, a slack-wire dog act.]

• • • • •

John: Pat [Kelly] works for us occasionally, out at the Hall of Fame.

Ruby: When he was a little kid, he painted our truck tires. We used to paint the elephants' toenails to go in the circus, and we had the paint sitting there, where the elephants go in. It was watercolor. Well, when they come out, why here he's got all of our tires painted on the truck! He was always doin' something. He was always into everything. Joe Lewis—his mother Eva [a trapeze aerialist] was married to Joe [Pat Kelly's stepfather]—she was always doin' something. With the cigarette hangin' out of her mouth, and she'd say, "Look here, girls!" and she'd be crocheting something, cigarette ashes all over it.

[All of Josephine's children are circus people. Myrna Timberlake uses the stage name Silverlake, as did her father, and operates a very successful dog act in Alaska. Jimmy Timberlake is the head of the Ringling "elephant retirement center" in Sarasota, Florida. Melvin "Cowboy Mel" Timberlake, who was a popular performer and trained horses and elephants, is working in circus concessions. Joey Timberlake works with Josephine as a "front door man," setting up the marquee and assuring the safety and security of the audience as it enters the big top.]

A Day in the Life of the Circus

From Tom Dunwoody interview with Sharon L. Smith

2 February 2000

IN **1934** THEY [HAGENBECK-WALLACE] PUT OUT THE BIGGEST CIRCUS EVER out of Peru. The Circus Hall of Fame Museum has an accurate miniature of that circus, down to the number of elephants and the sideshow banner line. It's made by guys who make circus miniatures, and it's all copied from old photographs. The owner was John Ringling that year, and the manager was Jess Adkins. Emmett Kelly, Otto Griebling, the Cristianis, all these famous people performed that year.

When the circus came to town, they paraded right down Main Street. Talk about an advertising stunt. Businesses closed, all the schools closed, everybody went to the circus. You can imagine, if you were in a small town back at the turn of the century or even later, most people never traveled out of the county. The big trip then was to go to the county seat. When the circus came to town, they had bands, they had wild animals, they had horses, they had pretty ladies, all coming down Main Street. It was just magical. It was the biggest thing ever to hit town. And that's why the circus was the biggest form of entertainment.

You had to have a lot of bands for the parade, so you took the big show band, which is about twenty to thirty guys, and you split them in two, and you put one half, the number one band, in the front in the bandwagon. They led the parade. There'd be guys with trumpets right out in front, and every time they'd turn a corner they'd give a fanfare and yell, "Hold your horses, here come the elephants!" Horses are definitely afraid of elephants. This was before there were a lot of cars, and of course there were horses lined all up and down Main Street.

The number two band, which is the other half of the big show band, you put them in a bandwagon four or five wagons behind the number one band, and four or five wagons after that they had a clown band. Then came the sideshow band, and they were black minstrels. Sometimes if they needed to, they would put together an all-woman band. Any of the performers who could play an instrument, they'd put them in. They needed a lot of music, since none of it makes any noise except for the horses and the wheels. The steam

calliope is always at the last because it scared the horses.

People today have no feel for how big the circus used to be. The lot the circus set up on was called the midway, with the big top in the middle and all these tents arranged around it. On the left-hand side was the sideshow. You had to pay extra to get into the sideshow. The sideshow had the fat lady, the giant, the midgets, and there were black minstrels in there. You had the snake charmers, the sword swallowers, and the Hawaiian dancers up on platforms—to attract the crowd. They called that "turning the tip." They had a hawker, who had a sign, and he'd get the people to pay twenty-five cents or whatever it was to get into the tent. Maybe they'd charge a dime or a quarter. Never very much. It wasn't a performance they did in the sideshow, you'd just walk around to each stage.

The circus would also carry a menagerie, and that tent would go on another side. Now the menagerie was free. The menagerie had thirty-two elephants in it in 1934 and exotic wild animals in cages. All the red cages had Clyde Beatty's lions and tigers, but the rest of them were various other animals. Down the middle of the tent they had the camels and the zebras, and they had a couple giraffes. This was bigger than most city zoos.

On the inside of the midway, near the big top, is the "pad room," or the dressing tent, with the ladies' dressing room on one side and the men's dressing room on the other side. To get to the big top, where they'd perform, the performers went across the "backyard," between the pad room and the big top. They also had a practice ring out in the middle of the lot.

THEY SET ALL OF THIS UP IN A DAY, AND THEN THEY HAD THE street parade, and then they gave an afternoon show and an evening show. They loaded it all back on the train that same day. They fed people three meals. The logistics are absolutely staggering. The big top was [an] arena for eight thousand people. Can you imagine moving that every day?

The secret of how they did it is so simple, yet so complicated. The manager, all he did was hire bosses. For every activity, there was a boss. First there was the train master. His only job was to load the train and get it to the next town and unload it. He was done for the day. Now if there was a flood, if there was a bridge out, it didn't matter, he had to get that train there regardless. So he knew the railroads intimately. He knew how to get around a train wreck or around a flood or whatever. Once he got the train unloaded, the boss hostler, who was in charge of the horses, his job was to get the wagons from the train to the lot. Once he got the wagons off the train, he was done for the day.

Then the boss canvas man took over, and his only job was to put up the big top. You've got to remember, it might be raining, there might be a foot of water, but they did the show anyway. The boss canvas man had maybe forty or fifty guys working for him. He had two or three assistants, and they got everybody into crews. It was kind of a military situation. In fact, Kaiser Wilhelm, when the Barnum and Bailey show was over in Europe for four years, he sent his general staff to follow the circus to figure out how they could move material and men that efficiently. All this was American equipment and American systems. You can just imagine the notes the military officers must've taken.

After the big top is set up, everybody goes and has breakfast. Then the property boss takes over. His only job was to set up the bleachers, the rings, and all the rigging. Then his job is done for the day. Then they do the parade, and they have a parade guy in charge of the parade. His only job was to make sure the parade happens. He's got to get a permit, he's got to get the parade route, he's got to make sure there are enough horses on each wagon, and so on.

Then it was time for the show, and that boss was called the equestrian director, what we think of as the ringmaster. Today they call him the performance director. He's in charge of everything in the big top. His word was law. He whistled an act down, and they came right down. They didn't argue with him. You had the same thing in the menagerie, you had a menagerie boss. They had a sideshow boss, or what they called the sideshow "talker." He would put together the sideshow. He hired the acts, got the banners painted up. They had an inside talker also. He would describe the fat lady, and the fire eater, and all of that. You had an electrical department—they carried their own generators and did their own electricity, so you had a boss of the electrical department. It just went on and on.

Each boss was just in charge of his area. I've talked to some of the old-timers, and they say that if you worked for the big top, you didn't encroach on the sideshow. Even the sideshow dog would not come over to the big top because they had a dog over there. They were very territorial.

The only guy who could call off the show was the big boss. The tent boss, or the hostler, or the railroad boss, they each say, "He's not going to call it off because of me." And see, that was the secret. Nobody was going to let down the show. They were so proud that if I'm the manager and I want to fire you, I say, "I think you ought to move that wagon over there about twenty feet." That boss would just turn and walk off the lot. Nobody tells you your job. Not even me, the big boss. That's how they fired guys. They knew they'd get a job the next day at another show. They lived circus all their lives. They're all gone now.

Hoosier Safari

Modoc the Elephant leads the authorities on a merry chase along the banks of the Wabash.

TERRELL JACOBS LEADS
ELEPHANT HUNT AT WABASH
Animal Frightened By Barking Dogs Starts On Rampage
WABASH, INDIANA, NOVEMBER 12, 1942—A gentle but stubborn female elephant named Modoc made the banks of the Wabash look like a Hollywood "Tarzan" set today, as the fleeing pachyderm led the pursuing safari a merry chase through six miles of river-bottom fields.

The county's first elephant-hunting expedition—minus the customary pith helmets—had Modoc snagged with a gaff hook three times today, but she shook loose, throwing two men off a bridge into the Wabash River for a dousing.

County Sheriff Vear Howell, who has a local reputation for trapping animals, got near enough to talk it over with Modoc. Some weeks ago, Howell was called upon to find a lost turkey. He gobbled effectively, won that turkey's confidence, and brought it back alive. "Modoc," he called sweetly. The ponderous hoofs skidded to a stop.

Modoc looked serenely back at Howell, then charged away again.

Modoc led an all-night chase that started yesterday when three elephants of the Great American Circus bolted during their performance at Wabash High School gymnasium when barking dogs frightened them. "Empress" and "Judy" were captured a few blocks from the school, but Modoc cut a swath through back yards and drug stores.

Terrell Jacobs of Peru, Indiana, the lion tamer who trained the elephants, described the renegade Modoc as "good natured," and state troopers said they would try not to destroy the animal today. Modoc has not shown rage, but simply refuses to go back home like a good girl. Jacobs took the calm sister pachyderms along on the chase, hoping they would lure Modoc into the fold.

Meanwhile, she had covered almost six miles at Lagro, Indiana, a little town of 542 terrorized souls. "A lot of fellows in the taverns swore off drinking when they saw an elephant charging around town," said Deputy Sheriff Paul Williams. Unbelieving farmers feared some prehistoric monster had come out of the hills. Lagro children were locked in without recess as they gazed wild-eyed from the windows, eager to join the chase. The erratic Modoc, meanwhile, was criss-crossing the Wabash river as if it were a sidewalk puddle. Jacobs feared she would bog down in the mud and "it would be an engineering feat to get her out."

At Wabash yesterday, Modoc lumbered into the basement garage of Jess Owens' home and blithely tore out the furnace and water pipes. Frightened residents ran helter-skelter before her. One woman, Mrs. Chauncey Kessler, 50, a housewife, ducked into Bradley Bros. drug store through whose open door came the smell of roasted peanuts. Modoc smelled, brought her 2,000 pounds to bear against the door, and followed Mrs. Kessler, who hid behind a counter. Modoc pushed over the soda fountain, tables and chairs and a glass display case. Waving her trunk, she picked up Mrs. Kessler, then gently put her down again and nudged her along with her feet. Mrs. Kessler was treated for minor cuts and bruises.

By this time, Jacobs and six of his helpers were trailing Modoc.

They were joined by Chief of Police Frank S. Gurtner and Wabash officers. But Modoc crashed through the back door of the store and headed for the outskirts of town. On the way she chased Arthur Stuart and knocked Ezra La Salle into his yard before trampling his grass. From there the trail led through the spacious residential district and across the gently rolling greens of the Wabash Country Club. The elephant hunters were joined by state police in four squad cars and more than 50 volunteers. But Modoc escaped through the sycamores along the Wabash River. At 10 p.m. the volunteers were called back because Jacobs believed they excited Modoc.

Jacobs, Gurtner, and a handful of searchers continued the elephant hunt. The spoor led them out of the woods along the hilly, brush-covered Wabash valley toward Lagro, six miles east. The trail was lost until early this morning, when the police department began receiving complaints from farmers that their cows, horses, and other stock were panic stricken and running loose over the countryside through broken fences. One startled farmer reported seeing a "monster" cross his pasture.

"It's an elephant," desk Sergeant Fred Aukerman explained.

"Well, whatever it was," the farmer replied, "my cows don't like it. They hightailed it off in the opposite direction when they saw it."

—*from the* Kokomo Tribune, *13 November 1942*

MODOC STILL ROAMS LOOSE, AND SHE'S NO ELEPHANTOM!

Peripatetic Pachyderm Invades Cornfield
And Breaks Up Shucking Party In Hurry

HUNTINGTON, INDIANA, NOVEMBER 14, 1942—Modoc, the moody and meandering elephant, still has her freedom. She was trapped today, but she untrapped herself. She was coaxed, cajoled, entreated, lured and implored to return to her security with the other elephants owned by Terrell and Dolly Jacobs, but she intends to live alone and like it.

But plans are being made to thwart her desire for solitude. The handsomest male elephant in all Indiana will be brought here tomorrow in the hope that he will be able to coax her back into captivity.

PNEUMONIA FEARED.

All other efforts to capture Modoc have failed, and it is feared that if she continues to stay out all day and all night she may get frostbite or pneumonia.

Early today, she put in her appearance before two brothers, Lloyd and Claude Krieg, who live near Mt. Etna, about 10 miles south of Huntington. They were shucking corn and talking about the beast that had been prowling through the neighborhood ever since she ran away Wednesday. At first Lloyd thought, "That's no elephant, that's an elephantom." But when Modoc raised her trunk and opened her mouth, both Lloyd and Claude knew exactly what to do.

THEY SET OUT IN A HURRY.

"We had the auto in the cornfield," said Lloyd, "and there was a trailer hitched onto her for the corn. I says to Claude, 'Walk, don't run,' and so we walked as far as the car. But as soon as the car started rolling, we didn't think of saving gas, or tires, or anything of the kind. Maybe we made 59 or 60 miles an hour getting out of that cornfield."

About this time, Indiana state police, under the direction of John C. Morgan, were searching the woods and the banks along the Salamonie River and questioning residents of farmhouses. Policeman James D. Armond, tramping along the north bank and scanning every inch of the ice-encrusted path, finally came upon the elephant's tracks. They went up a high cliff and across Highway No. 9 toward the east.

POLICE SPEED TO FARM.

Armond got into his car in time to hear the radio from headquarters instructing him to proceed one mile east and then a mile north. Within a few minutes he and a half dozen other policemen had pulled into the driveway of the Krieg farm.

"Block this road," Morgan ordered. "Don't let anybody pass. Maybe we can get this creature today if we haven't a crowd."

—from the Chicago Sun, 15 November 1942
By Eddie Doherty, Staff Correspondent.

MODOC IS HOME
HEALTH IS BETTER

Elephant That Created Excitement For Four Days Is Captured

PERU, INDIANA, NOVEMBER 20, 1942—Modoc, the wayward elephant, who for four days wanted to be alone, changed her attitude late Sunday afternoon and welcomed visitors who led her back to captivity and regimented life.

The ponderous pachyderm was captured on the farm of Lloyd Krieg near Mount Etna, Huntington County, where for two days she had been resisting attempts of deputy sheriffs, farmers, and circus men to get her inside a large circus truck. Her two elephant playmates, Judy and Empress, assisted in the capture.

DOCILE AS A KITTEN.

Judy and several persons, including Terrell Jacobs, owner of the three elephants, walked up to Modoc in the Krieg woods, and after Jacobs had given Modoc 30 loaves of bread and Judy had trumpeted pleadingly, Modoc walked with her into the truck. Empress, chained inside the truck, waited patiently until Modoc strolled in with Judy.

Earlier in the afternoon, Sheriff Marvin Idle of Huntington County had given Modoc 30 other loaves of bread while Mr. Jacobs put a large leather harness around her and fastened the harness to a chain which had been attached securely to a tree. Modoc didn't seem to mind the harness while she was eating, but after she completed her meal she broke out of it with ease and lumbered about in the woods. Then the successful harness-less method of capture was decided upon.

Modoc and the other two animals were brought in the truck to their home southwest of Peru on Federal Highway 31.

TAKES NAP IN ROAD.

Modoc, who spent nearly all of Friday in a thicket in a low section of the Krieg farm, ventured within 20 feet of the Krieg home late Friday night and then wandered into a county road bordering the farm. She lay down in the middle of the road for awhile and Indiana state police from the Ligonier post placed red warning lanterns about her. Shortly before dawn, the pachyderm established her headquarters in the woods in which she received visitors in the afternoon.

Thousands of Hoosiers, who sought a glimpse of the elephant whose escapades have brought her nation-wide fame, flocked to the Krieg farm Sunday, but were turned away by state police, who established numerous road barricades. Some 200 persons who reached the farm on foot were warned to keep away from the woods.

LOSES 800 POUNDS IN WEIGHT.

Great misgivings about Modoc's health were expressed Sunday by Mr. Jacobs, who said that the two-ton circus performer probably had lost as much as 800 pounds in weight.

"Elephants require a huge amount of water," he said, "and I believe Modoc had obtained practically none since she started her journey. Of course, she crossed the Wabash and Salamonie rivers, but I think she was too frightened at that time to stop and drink. Modoc didn't have much food, either. Contrary to popular belief, she was unable to forage for enough food to meet her requirements."

KEEPER LOOKS TO ANIMAL'S HEALTH.

One of the first steps to be taken by Mr. Jacobs in restoring Modoc to good health was to give her no less than six quarts of whiskey, he said.

Once Modoc had lumbered into the truck the deputy sheriff, farmers and circus men sighed deeply, but there was no cheering, a general belief being that Modoc would tear her way out of the truck if she were startled. All the members of the safari were unusually tired. Mr. Jacobs in particular was jubilant. He values Modoc at $6,000.

—from the Peru Republican, 20 November 1942.

MODOC DRINKS WARM WATER AND EATS BRAN MASH

After Four-Day Spree; Ready For Show Soon

PERU, INDIANA, NOVEMBER 16, 1942—(AP)—Modoc, a 14-year-old Indian elephant, whose antics exhausted a safari of Indianans in a four-day chase along the Wabash river, munched contentedly today within a huge animal barn on the Terrell Jacobs farm five miles south of Peru.

Modoc swayed to and fro in her stall, carrying on a continuous trunk-to-mouth consumption of gallons of luke warm water and copious amounts of bran mash. Jacobs explained his elephant would soon regain approximately 800 pounds lost while she was loose. "She shows no reaction to the chase otherwise," Jacobs said. "However, she still is a little nervous. Otherwise, she's as normal as she'll ever be." Jacobs added that "she'll be ready to take to the road again" the latter part of this week with her two sister elephants Empress and Judy. The three were shipped by a dealer from Burma in 1938, and all are natives of India.

Jacobs admitted that despite his assurances that Modoc was "nearly back to normal, Mrs. Jacobs won't let our boy (Terrell Jr., aged 3 and ½) go down to the barn to feed Modoc." He said the boy often played with the elephant.

The Jacobs farm consists of 14 and ½ acres, a mile and a half west of nearby Bunker Hill. In addition to the herd of elephants he has 27 lions, tigers, leopards, kangaroos and llamas. Jacobs, who has been in circus and animal work for 26 years, added that during Modoc's absence the farm had a new arrival—a baby llama.

—*from the* Kokomo Tribune, *17 November 1942.*

MEMORY OF "MODOC" LIVES ON

As Case Is Set For Trial

ROCHESTER, INDIANA, JANUARY 5, 1943—Judge Kline Reed in Fulton circuit court today set down for trial on March 19 before a jury the $10,000 damage suit of Mrs. Grace Kessler of Wabash against Terrell Jacobs, famous wild animal trainer of Peru and others.

Mrs. Kessler in her suit for damages alleges that Modoc forced his way into a drug store in Wabash where she was a customer and attacked her. The plaintiff says the elephant tossed her to the floor with his trunk and then trampled her. For injuries which she alleges she received, Mrs. Kessler asks the $10,000 damages.

—*from the* Logansport Press, *6 January 1945*

THE JACOBS DIVORCE CASE

The meandering Hoosier elephant, Modoc, the best-known female pachyderm in at least three Indiana counties, popped back into the news Tuesday. But she only made circus and marital news this time—not the black headlines she garnered as the terrifying mad elephant of the Wabash valley.

Now, Modoc is the pawn of a divorce action. She and her two sisters, Empress and Judy, are included in the personal property awarded to Mrs. Dolly Jacobs as receiver in divorce court. Jacobs retained sixteen lions and several camels and elephants from his menagerie. His wife was awarded the two elephants, a lion, two horses, a Great Dane, and a steel arena for a lion act.

Mrs. Jacobs' attorney said she had 32 weeks' booking and will have a rival show to that of her husband.

And Modoc will probably be the feature attraction of the new circus.

—*from the* Peru Republican, *2 March 1943*

MAN INJURED BY ELEPHANT ASKS
$25,000 DAMAGES

Huntington Resident Plaintiff In Action Against Terrell Jacobs

Modoc, a capricious elephant which has the capacity of winning newspaper headlines, and whose custody is now being sought through a divorce petition, was back in the news again Thursday, this time by means of a $25,000 damage action for alleged injuries suffered when trampled by the animal. The damage action was filed Thursday morning by Kenneth A. Kindley against Terrell Jacobs and Marie Jacobs, owners of Modoc and other wild animals, and J.

CLYDE
BEATTY-COLE
BROS.
CIRCUS
SOUTH BEND
4-H FAIR GROUNDS
Auspices: Avalon Grotto
SAT. AND SUN.
AUG.
19
AND
20
SAT. AFT. & NITE - SUN. 2 & 5:30

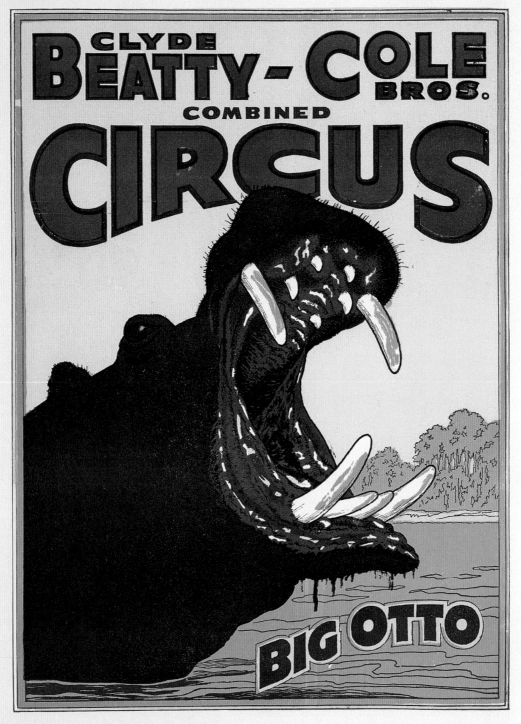

Lyman Keyes of the American Amusement Company, which had a contract with the Jacobs' to exhibit the animals.

After the elephant had escaped from his trainers in Wabash it made the farm of Glen Burnett, on which the plaintiff was employed, a port of call. When he discovered that the animal had visited the farm, Kindley says he made a tour of inspection to determine if any of the livestock on the farm had been harmed. When he neared the thicket where the elephant was standing, he saw his father a short distance away examining a fence, and called to warn him of the elephant's nearness. When the animal heard the shout, he says, it charged on him, knocking him to the ground and trampling him.

—*from the* Peru Tribune, *7 September 1944*

MODOC REFORMS JUNGLE WAYS TOP PERFORMER

CHICAGO, APRIL 30, 1943—An open letter to the folks on the Wabash:

REMEMBER MODOC, that wayward elephant? Remember how she ran away from a school performance, rampaged through a drug store, frightened a whole town, then wallowed through the cornfields on the banks of the Wabash for four days last year?

Well, we called on Modoc today at the Olympia Circus and found that she had reformed her jungle ways. She had acquired polish during the winter—at least red toenail polish—and she's a star performer. Her owner, Terrell (Terry) Jacobs, calls her "Terry's little lamb."

"She's a model lamb, too," he said. "Modoc's not the tomboy she used to be. She's a little lady now." Modoc had just been dancing like a pachyderm Pavlova in the circus ring a few minutes before we met her. "Our best dancer, too," Jacobs said. Modoc stretched out her trunk and affectionately twined it around Jacobs' neck. "The last five months have done things to Modoc. She has come into her own."

No fooling, Modoc is the glamour girl of the elephants. No ugly wrinkles, no projecting ribs, no loose epidermis. Modoc is a smoothie—not too fat, not too lean. Sturdy, but not too sturdy—about perfect in a pachyderm sort of way, at least we thought so, though we don't pretend to be a judge of elephant beauty.

The opening of the circus season this year was like a coming out party for her, Jacobs said. She is just 16, but her growing-up process that ended in her present charm began last November after her last great fling along the Wabash. She has been attending school since at Jacobs' Peru, Indiana farm and even did her bit of war work this spring by plowing the fields for the 1943 Victory crops and pulling wagons. "That affair last fall," Jacobs said, "was just a kiddish thing. After all, that's all she was then, just a kid. You'd know better now, wouldn't you, Mo?"

Mo's trunk dropped. She swayed with elephantine grace. Her eyes were tranquil. We patted her downcast, forest-brown head and we know you'd have done so too, because Terry's little lamb is no black sheep now.

Sincerely Yours,
GWEN MORGAN
U.P. Staff Correspondent
—*from the* Peru Daily Tribune, *30 April 1943*

MODOC UPSETS STAND, CHAINED

Modoc, one of six elephants owned by local circus man Terrell Jacobs, who has been appearing with the Olympia Circus in the Chicago stadium, was temporarily retired from circulation Sunday afternoon after she charged out of the arena into the lobby, where she upset a refreshment stand before being led away in chains.

Terrell Jacobs said she may be returned to the circus farm near Twin Bridges for a rest.

—*from the* Peru Tribune, *17 April 1944*

• • • • •

Modoc was awarded to Marie (Dolly) Jacobs in the divorce. The elephant continued to perform in the circus until her death in 1960.